All the buildings you can build during your adventure are listed in the Bui[...] them. For example, you will not be able to build a Small Prison before buil[...] have at least $200.

Let's imagine you decide to build the Blacksmith. First, deduct $200 from your Bank Account. Next, look at your map, which is divided into squares. According to the Building Registry, the Blacksmith takes up one square on the ground. You can build it wherever you want on your map as long as you have sufficient land. At the beginning of your adventure, you can only build in the section labeled "Town Zone". You will be able to buy or trade for the other territories (Zones) as you progress through the adventure.

When placing buildings, you must follow the following rules: First, you must build within the predesignated squres. Building on rivers, mountains, or outside of the grid is not allowed. Second, each building must have at least one side facing the street. For example, you cannot build a lot of 3 buildings by 3 since the house in the middle will not have access to the street. These rules will be explained in more detail as you progress through your adventure.

After building the Blacksmith and filling in a single square on your map, you create a new job: check one box on the **Jobs** table. The Blacksmith gives you one Safety point and two Approval points, so check the appropriate number of boxes on the **Safety** and **Approval** tables. Finally, add the $50 that the Blacksmith will give you each month to the **Monthly Income** section.

At any time and if you have the necessary resources, you can build a new building and place it on your map. Thanks to your carrier falcon, you can order work on a building site without needing to physically be in town. Progress, amiright? And since we're in a book, we can do as we please: building is instantaneous! Residents work the same way. If you build a house, a resident will automatically come to Your Town.

A word of caution if you lose a building (yes, that will most likely happen): you lose all of its bonuses (Monthly Income, Approval, Population, etc.). Don't forget to track this on the tables in your Ledger.

Also note that some buildings will lose money each month (school, prison, etc.). The sum shown in the Monthly Income column of the Building Registry will thus need to be deducted from your Monthly Income.

**QUICK HINT** : To make identifying your buildings on the map easier, assign them an initial or an icon. For example, identify a bank with $, draw a cross for a cemetery, a stick figure for a house, etc.

## MYSTERIES

Whenever a panel contains this icon, it means that a mystery is present. This might be a riddle to solve or a puzzle to decipher. Often times the solution to the mystery will not be obvious, and solving it may require you to have found a hint or clue elsewhere. Each mystery has a different colored icon, allowing you to quickly determine if you've found the solution simply by checking the icons. **Don't cheat!** Solving the mysteries on your own is one of the most satisfying aspects of the game.

## EVENTS 🎖

Starting with the third month of your adventure, each time you see a circled letter at the top of a panel, make a note of your current panel and then visit panel **102** to discover which event happens in Your Town. Afterwards, return to the panel you were previously at. You may gain or lose money, population, or various points. However, you can never have a negative value.

## OBJECTS

During your adventure, you can pick up any object you see, as long as it's not on someone. Some of these objects will not be of any use, but you won't know for sure. As long as you have space, take whatever isn't nailed down and make a note of it in your **Notes** box. Consequently, if you find an object, you can only pick it up during your first pass through.

If you haven't yet started your adventure and this is your first time playing, now is the time to turn the page and begin (don't worry, you'll return here later to choose a mission objective). Otherwise, choose the objective you wish to attempt to complete. The number of stars indicates the mission's difficulty level. If you succeed, at the end of the game you will multiply your points by the difficulty level of your mission. Once you've chosen your mission, return to 88 to make your first decisions.

- ☐ Build at least 5 buildings in Zone D ⭐
- ☐ Build 15 different buildings ⭐
- ☐ Have a Population of at least 100 ⭐
- ☐ Complete the adventure without cheating ⭐
- ☐ Build a School, a Hospital, a Large Prison, and a Town Hall ⭐⭐
- ☐ Have a Population of at least 150 ⭐⭐

- ☐ Have a Monthly Income of $3000 ⭐⭐
- ☐ Build at least 2 buildings in each Zone ⭐⭐⭐
- ☐ Have an Approval rating of 100 ⭐⭐⭐
- ☐ Own all Zones ⭐⭐⭐
- ☐ Have Monthly Income of $5000 ⭐⭐⭐
- ☐ Build all the buildings on the Building Registry ⭐⭐⭐

If you're a young reader or wish to play a shorter and simpler game, you may ignore the events, you have unlimited bullets, and you start your adventure with $500 in your Bank Account!

**Author:** Shuky / **Illustration:** 2D / **Translation:** JF Gagné
This book is a translation of the original *Your Town* © Makaka Éditions

© Van Ryder Games 2018

All Rights Reserved. No part of this publication may be reproduced, stored in a retrieval system, or transmitted, in any form or by any means, without the prior written permission of Van Ryder Games.

Van Ryder Games and Graphic Novel Adventures are Trademarks of Van Ryder Games LLC
ISBN : 978-0-9997698-3-6    Library of Congress Control Number: 2018933574

Published by Van Ryder Games and printed in China by Long Pack

Find printable game sheets and other Graphic Novel Adventures at **www.vanrydergames.com**

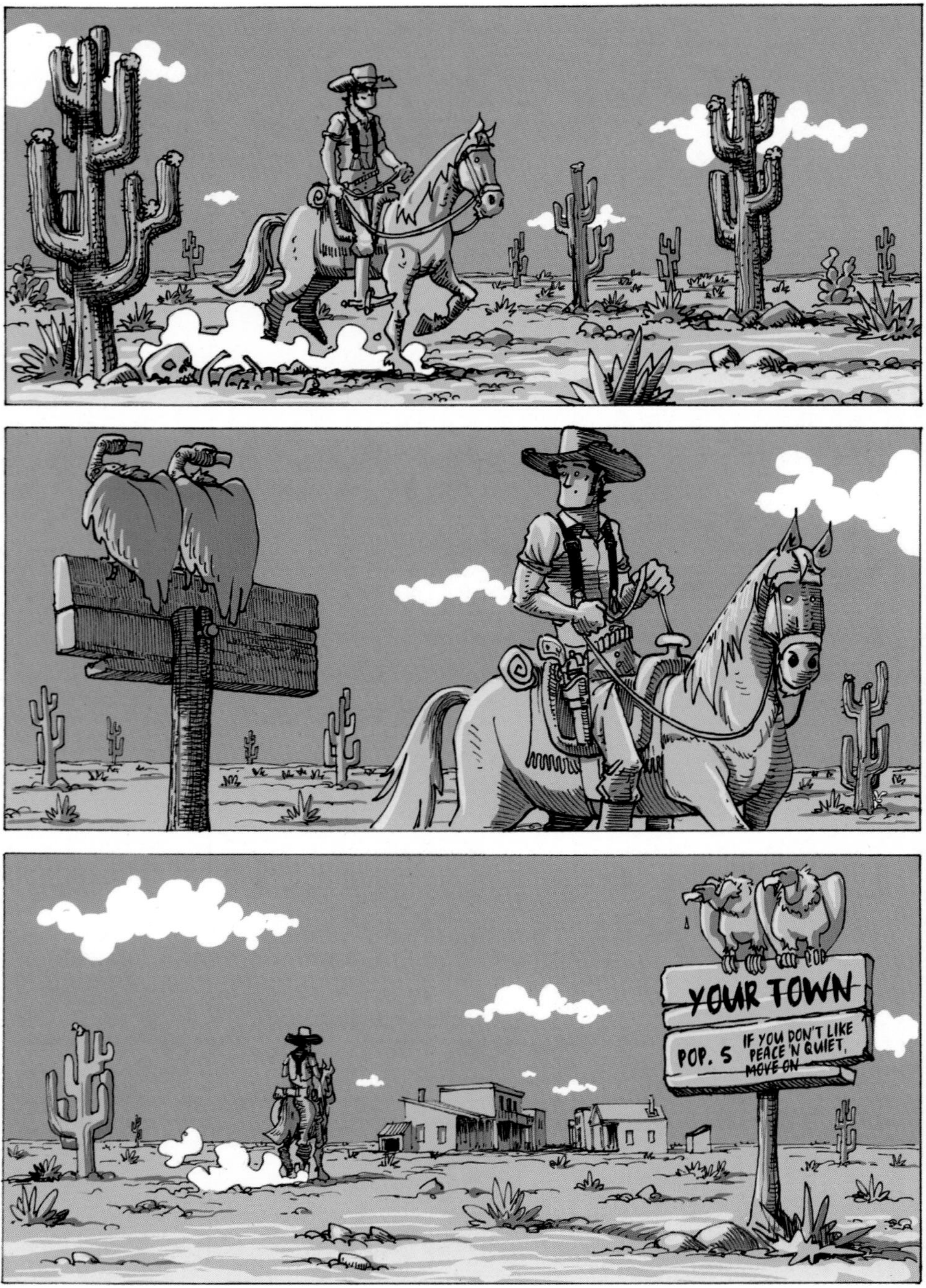
YOUR TOWN
POP. 5
IF YOU DON'T LIKE PEACE 'N QUIET, MOVE ON

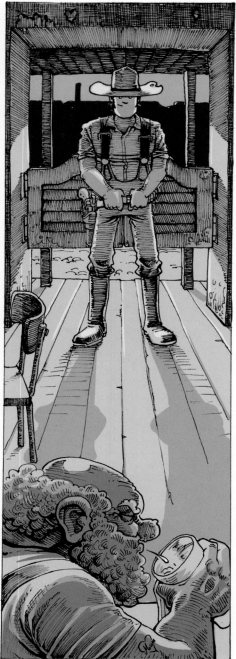

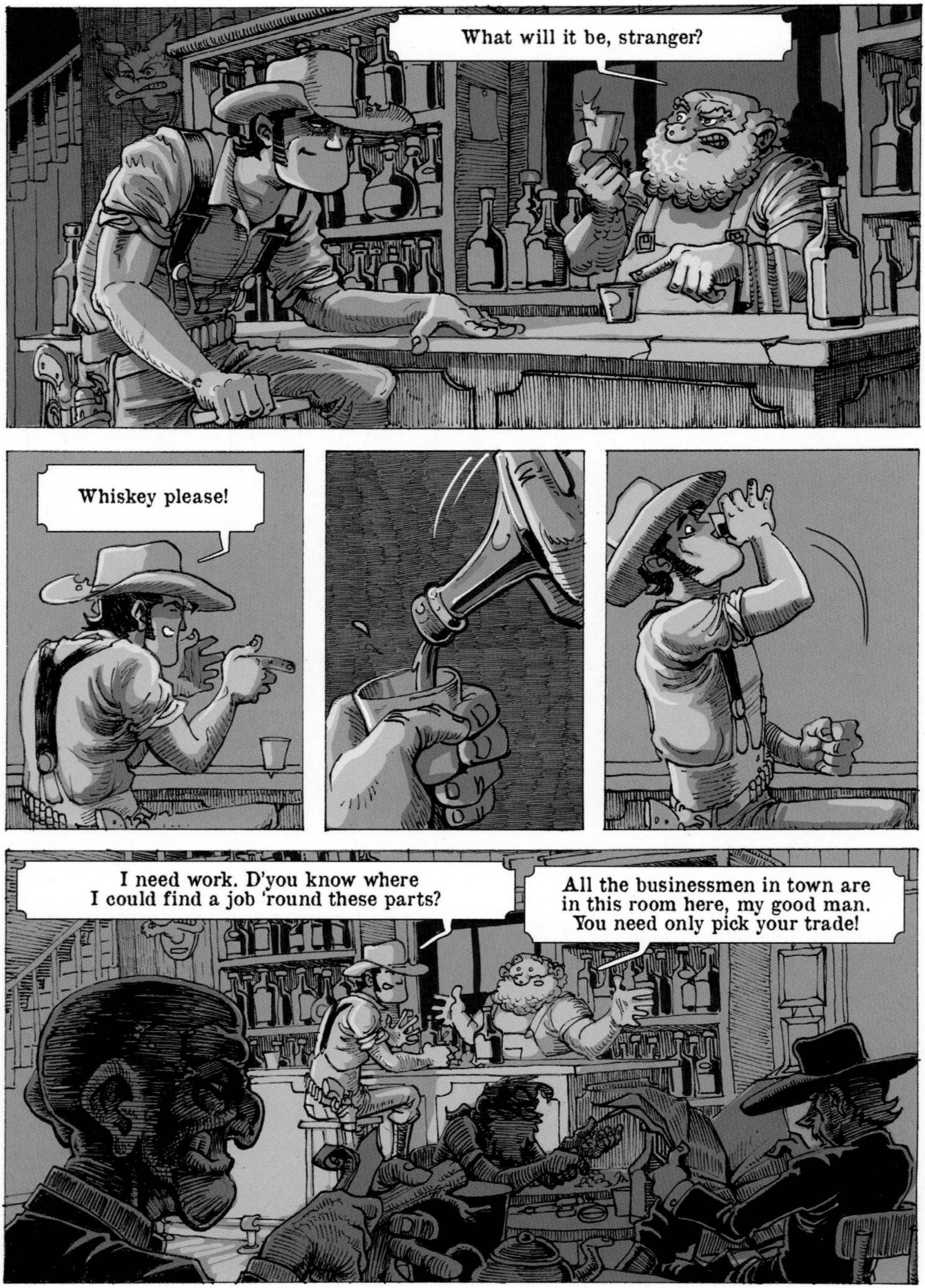
What will it be, stranger?
Whiskey please!
I need work. D'you know where I could find a job 'round these parts?
All the businessmen in town are in this room here, my good man. You need only pick your trade!

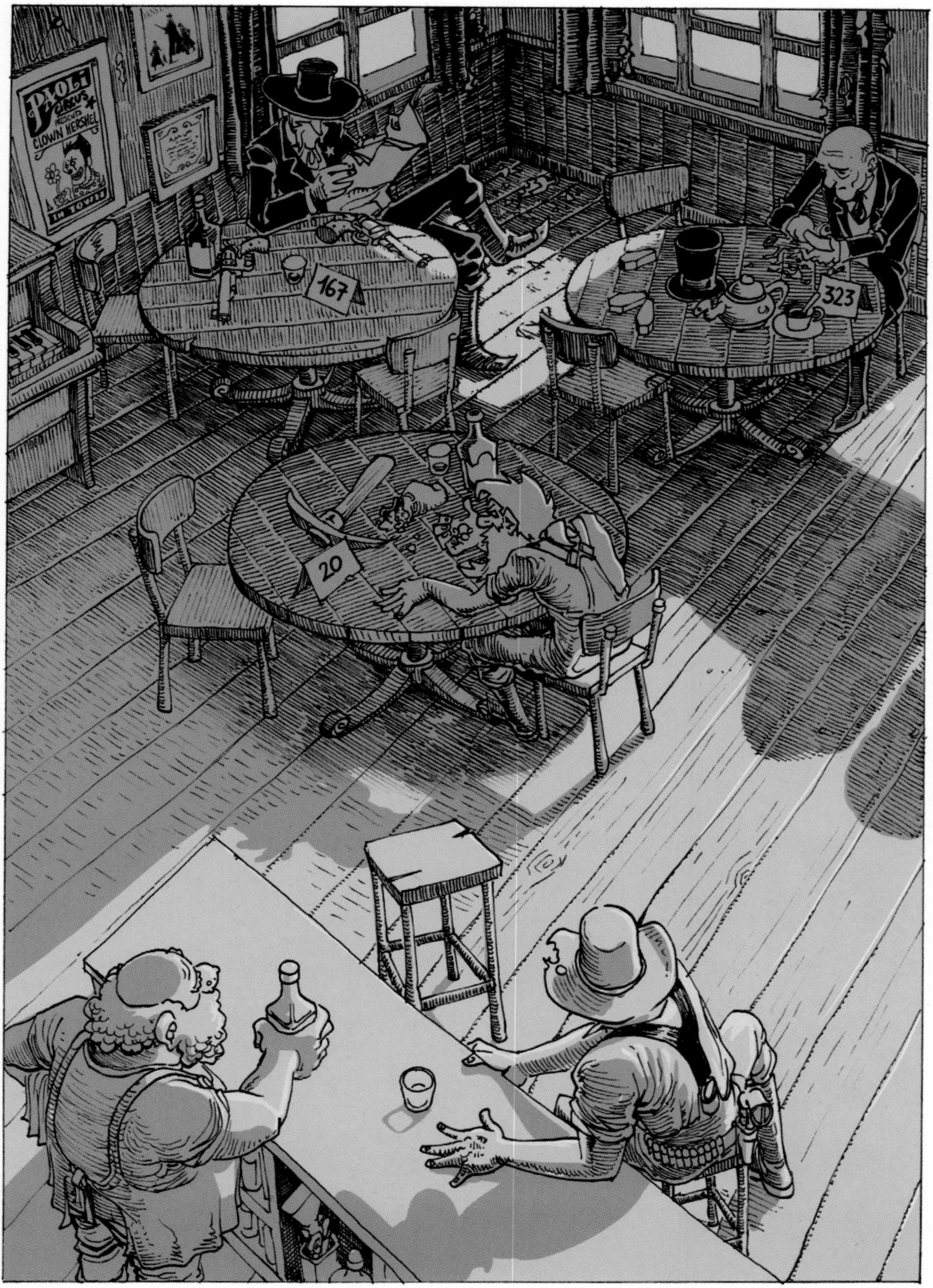
PIOLI
CIRCUS
PRESENTS
CLOWN HERSHEL
IN TOWN
167
323
20

**1**

So, time for a little review. It appears that building a **School** was one of your most popular decisions. According to the latest surveys, your Approval went up 15 points. This number is doubled if you managed to hire two teachers. Furthermore, it seems that one of the school's students, little Nathan, is particularly gifted. He's developed a **Mill** that can produce flour and feed 20 people.

After noting down all of this, go back to 88. As you know, you won't be able to visit the Engineer until another month has passed. Note that the **Mill** takes two squares by two squares on your map and costs nothing to build.

**2**

Dear Mister Mayor,

During your sudden absence (quite unexpected, if I say so myself), I took upon myself to take care of the administrative tasks. Without your skills, I regret to inform you that I made a few small mistakes.

In short, we lost $450. 2 residents and your Approval rating dropped 5 points.

Nevertheless, I wish you a wonderful day, Mr. Mayor.

Let's hope you will learn from this! A Mayor shouldn't leave his town to deliver beer! Time to return to your office in 88.

**3**

That's quite the eye you've got! You've just found an iron ore deposit. If this land belongs to you, you may build an **Iron Mine** here. Go back to 17.

**4**

If you made it here without cheating, go see the engineer at his office in 135. Otherwise, return to Page 7 so as not to spoil your adventure.

**5**

Puma tracks. You'd better be on your guard. Draw your weapon and continue to 18, or go back to your office in 88.

**6**

Well, well! That one was tough to spot. Nice shot cowboy! Go to 85.

**7**

What do you want from me? I did nothing wrong. I ain't robbed no one!

If you want to have this man arrested, go to 52. If you wish to play Bluff with him, go to 188. If you'd rather let him off the hook, go to 30.

**8**

'Course I know who these lands belong to... they're mine! I'm willing to sell them to ya for $1500. In'erested?

If you have a good (G) relationship with McKenzie, head to 308 to negotiate the final price. Otherwise, you can still buy the land within Zone F for $1500. You will be able to construct all building types there. Whether or not you buy Zone F, make your way to 333 or return to your office in 88.

Hold your pencil approximately 6 inches high and drop it over your enemy. You only get one shot (unless otherwise indicated by a special weapon or bonus, etc.). If you hit your enemy, you win and can go to 85. If you miss, go to 179.

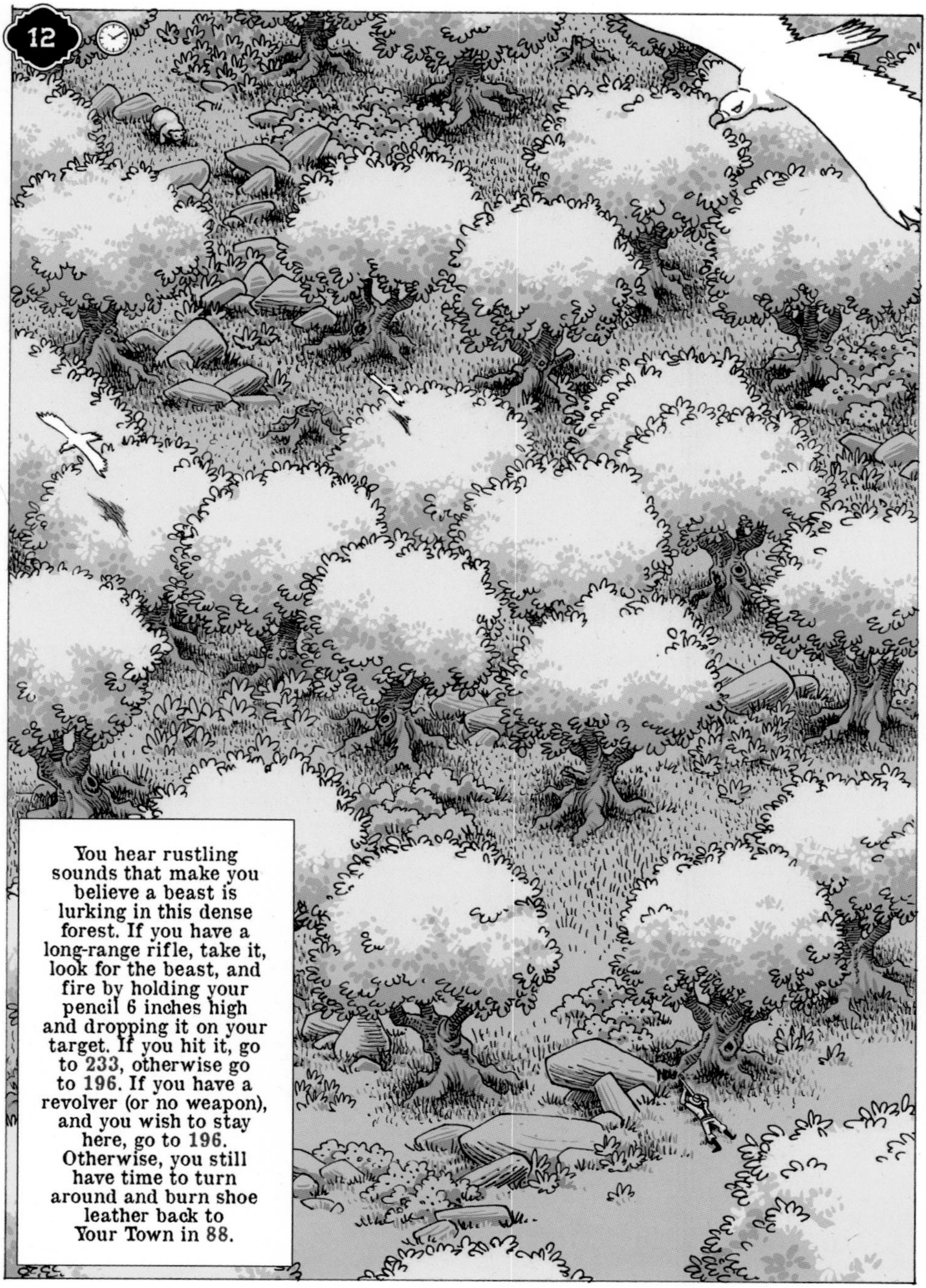
12
You hear rustling sounds that make you believe a beast is lurking in this dense forest. If you have a long-range rifle, take it, look for the beast, and fire by holding your pencil 6 inches high and dropping it on your target. If you hit it, go to 233, otherwise go to 196. If you have a revolver (or no weapon), and you wish to stay here, go to 196. Otherwise, you still have time to turn around and burn shoe leather back to Your Town in 88.

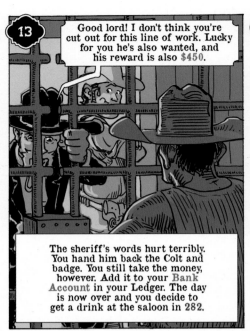

**13** Good lord! I don't think you're cut out for this line of work. Lucky for you he's also wanted, and his reward is also $450.

The sheriff's words hurt terribly. You hand him back the Colt and badge. You still take the money, however. Add it to your Bank Account in your Ledger. The day is now over and you decide to get a drink at the saloon in 282.

**14** Thank you for the letter! A friend of mine wanted me to move to Your Town. If you have a Motel, I could work there...

If you have a Motel in your town, Mauricette joins you. She'll build her Small House on her own dime and the Motel will earn you an extra $100 each month. Otherwise, you will have to leave this pretty lady on the side of the road and head back to your office in 88.

**15** Well, look at Mister Big Head Mayor here. You've forgotten where you're from! Don't set foot in my saloon ever again!

Your friendship with Jackman just took a hit. Note in your Ledger that your relationship is bad (B), then return to 88.

**16** Hey Mister Mayor! You plannin' on building a Stagecoach Station? If you are, I'd love to work there. I could even use my cart to help you save some money.

If you have a Stagecoach Station and decide to hire Marty, the station will earn you an extra $100 per month and immediately grant you 2 Approval points. If you don't have a Stagecoach Station but want to build one, Marty helps out and it will only cost you $200. However, the bonuses will be the same as those found in the Building Registry. You may also decline his offer and return to your office in 88.

337

An enormous puma pounces on you. If your weapon was drawn, you react instantly and once again prove what a sharp shot you are. You can go to 322. If you did not have your weapon drawn, you manage to dodge the animal and run at a hell-for-leather pace back to your office in 88.

Someone is approaching you. You can turn back in 88 to avoid any confrontation. You can also head towards him in 320, or hide in 111 and take some time to decide.

... 875, 876, 877 ...

If you wish to ask this man for a job, go to 305. If you'd rather wait for him to finish counting his gold, go to 264. If, after all, you think his job does not look very captivating, return to Page 7 to choose a different trade.

**21**

**22**

Gringo, you may have nothin' to do but fart in the wind, but I've got work to do. Only another pint could keep me here a little longer...

...if you catch my drift.

You can pay drinks for everyone in 215 to keep the sheriff here, but this will cost you $50. Otherwise, you tip your hat to him and return to your office in 88.

**23**

Move along, chicken. Move along, I said!

You may go to 168.

**24**

WANTED
JOSEY WALES

WANTED
COBB
DEAD OR ALIVE
75 000 $

WAN
JOE

DEAD OR A
1 000 $

1 000

So, Mister Mayor, s'everything going according to plan? Well, I have a small mission for you. Here's a list of five wanted outlaws. If you meet them during your travels, take care of 'em. Permanently, if you catch my drift.

To see the list of wanted outlaws, go to 187.

**25** If you have some water, take a sip and go to 96. Otherwise, make your way to 254.

**26** You've just found a hidden treasure, which earns you $1000. It's your lucky day! Note it in your Ledger and then return where you were before and continue your adventure.

**27** Mmmkay... well I think there's more than just nuggets in there. But that's still good work you did. Here's $500 worth. Don't spend it all in one place now.

Note this reward under your Bank Account in your Ledger, then return to the saloon in 282.

**28**

**29** Good lord, I've never seen such poor shooting in all my life! Perhaps working with the Engineer in 47 is more your speed.

**30**

As soon as you exit the Casino, Fredo and his crew are back at the tables. Thanks to their swindling skills, they easily "rob" everybody. As result, the Casino and the town suffer a net loss of $800. Note this in your Ledger and then go back to your office in 88.

**31**

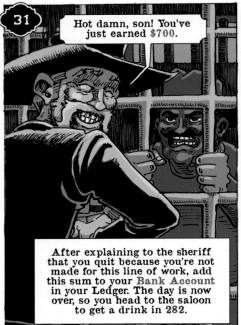

Hot damn, son! You've just earned $700.

After explaining to the sheriff that you quit because you're not made for this line of work, add this sum to your Bank Account in your Ledger. The day is now over, so you head to the saloon to get a drink in 282.

**32**

You...have better things to do, you say? I... yes, I understand.

This decision results in a loss of $500. It appears that Fredo Maxwell is in fact the captain of a formidable team of poker players. Their mission is to "rob" every player in the Casino, fairly. Among their victims are numerous town hall employees who gamble with their paychecks. You can now return to 88.

**33**

Good news, Mister Mayor! We found a new gold vein in one of your mines that we had believed to be exhausted. This will refill our coffers to the tune of $1000!

After noting down all of this, go back to 88. As you know, you won't be able to visit the Engineer until another month has passed.

**34**

Your assailant clearly does not intend on making peace with you. You can try to find him in 225 or head back to Your Town at full speed in 88.

**35** A bear was here recently. You can carefully follows its tracks by foot in 119, or turn back and discretely return to Your Town in 88.

**36** 316

**37** Puma claw marks! If you haven't crossed paths with it yet, draw your weapon, giving you the opportunity to fire three times if you encounter the animal. Make your way to 221 or 78.

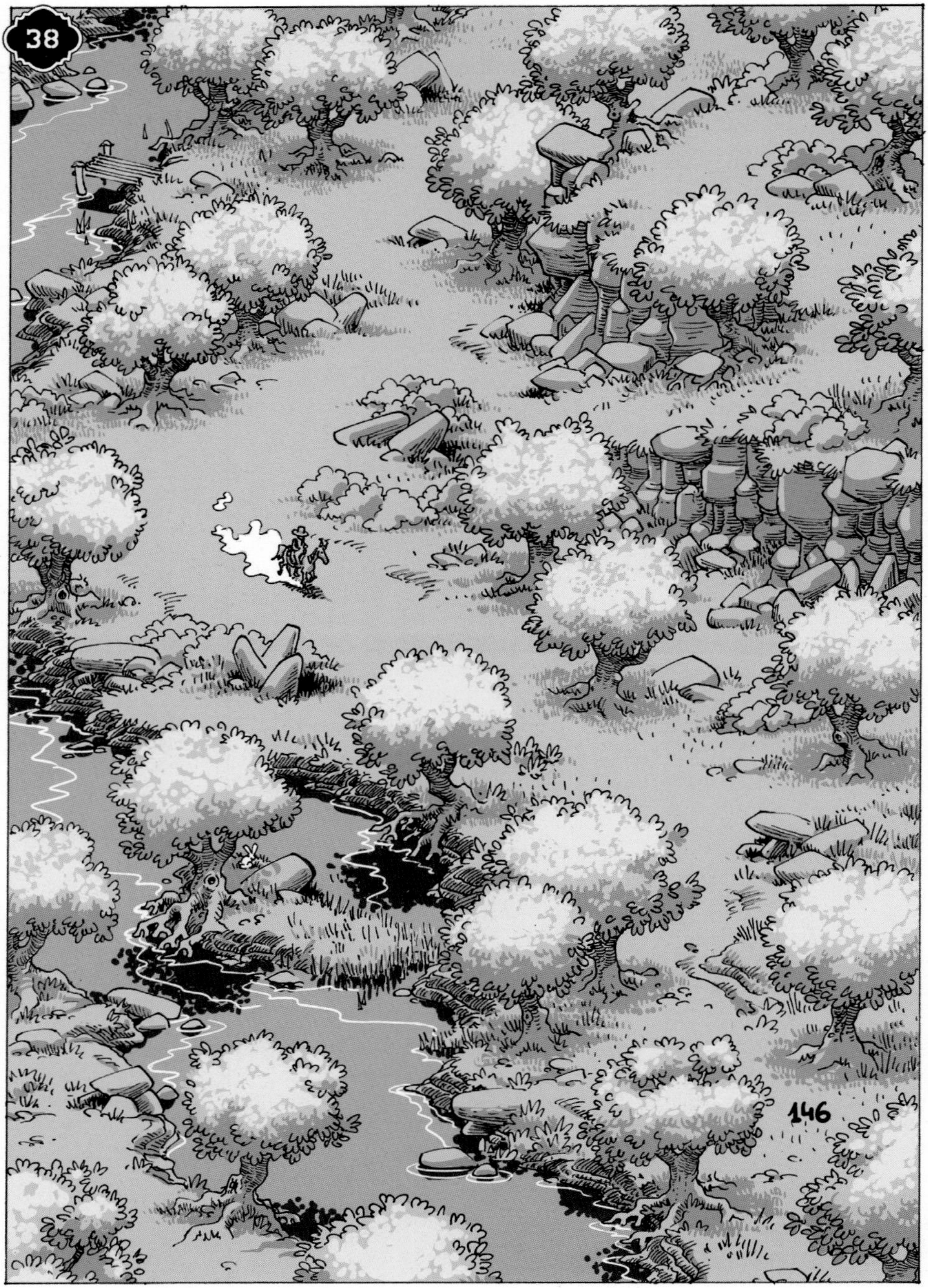
38
146

**39** The Prison...ah yes... well, it does grant you a higher Safety level, but sadly, your residents do not really appreciate having cattle thieves and other highwaymen for neighbors. Speaking of, one of the most infamous chicken thieves was released yesterday, and we suspect he is behind the disappearance of 10 hens. Needless to say, your Approval rating dropped 10 points. Additionally, you must reimburse the poor farmer for $50. Furthermore, if your Prison is next to a House or School, your Approval rating drops by an additional 10 points.

After writing down all of this, go back to 88. As you know, you won't be able to visit the Engineer until another month has passed.

**40** Join me at the shooting range in 185. Let's see what yer made of!

**41**

**42**

Apparently, he did not take you seriously. If Your Town has more work than population, or if your Approval rating is higher than 50, go to 302. Otherwise, silently finish your strawberry milk and leave this town, mocked by its citizens, before finally making it back to your office in 88.

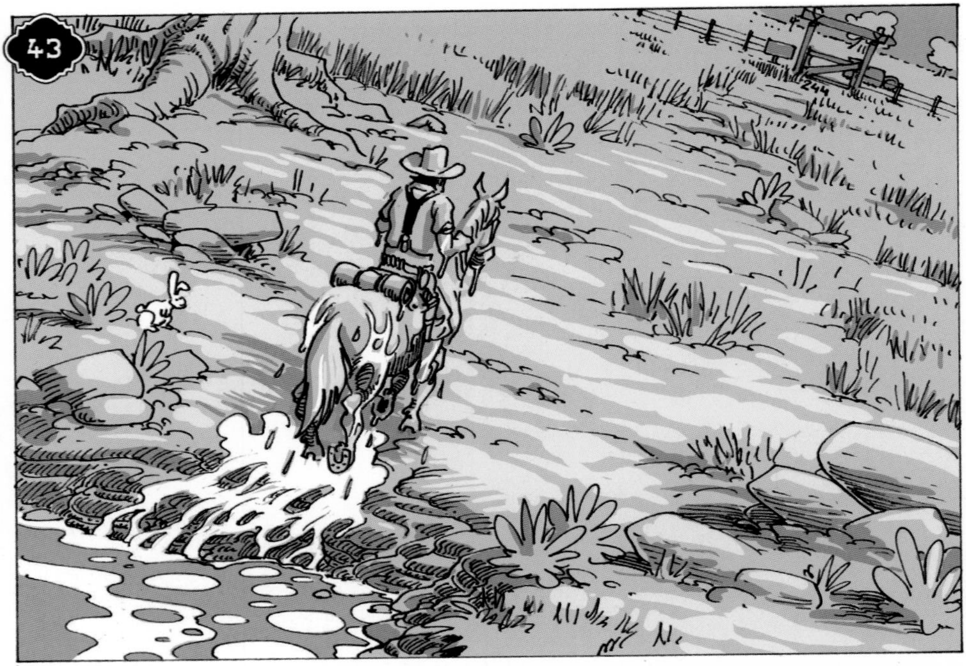
43
244

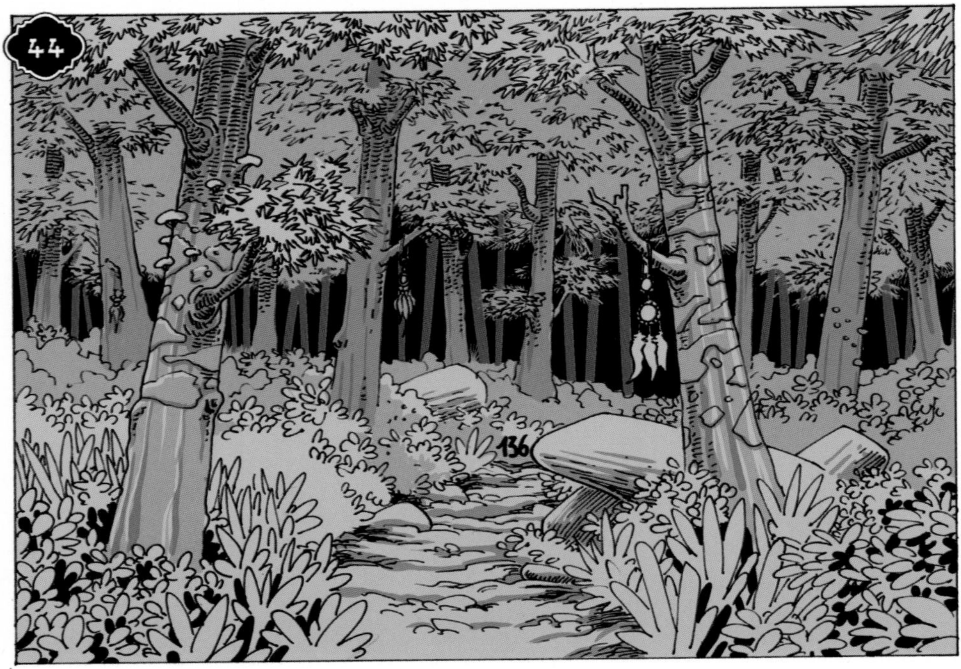
44
136

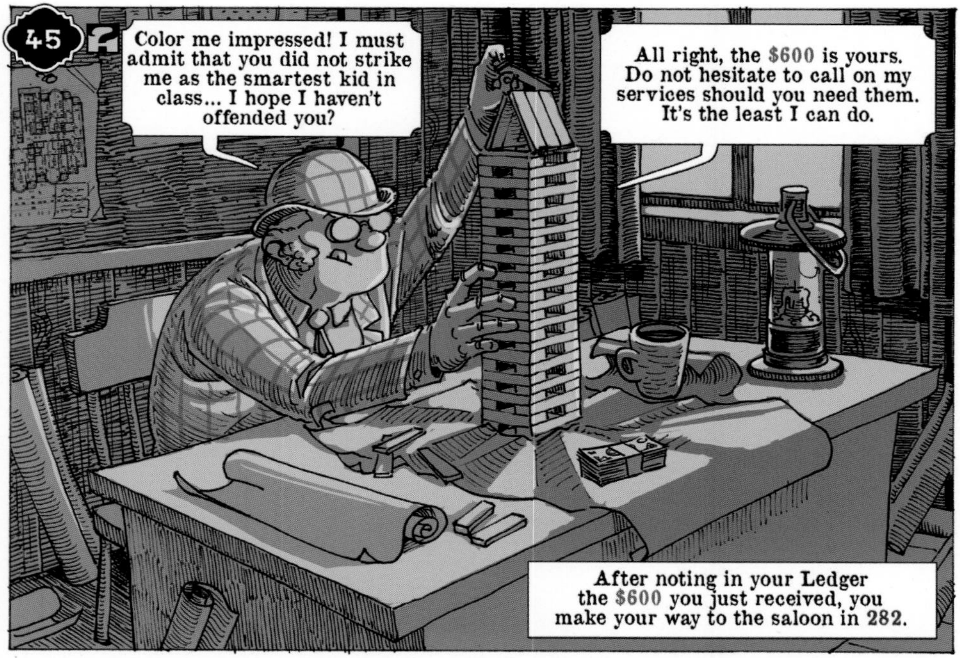
45
Color me impressed! I must admit that you did not strike me as the smartest kid in class... I hope I haven't offended you?
All right, the $600 is yours. Do not hesitate to call on my services should you need them. It's the least I can do.
After noting in your Ledger the $600 you just received, you make your way to the saloon in 282.

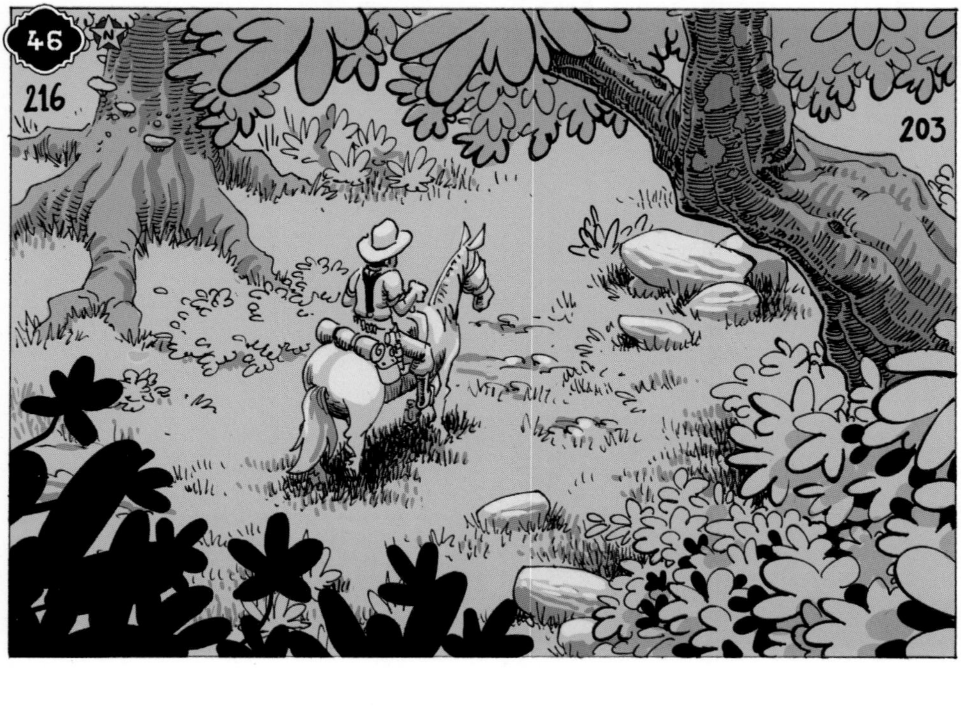
46
216
203

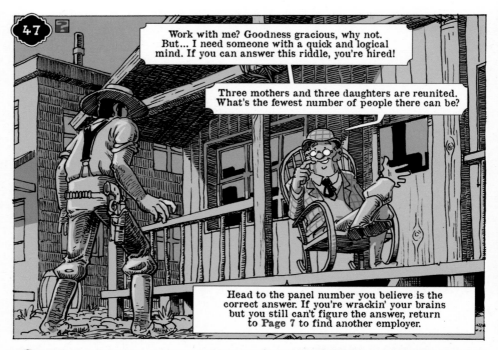

**47**

Work with me? Goodness gracious, why not. But... I need someone with a quick and logical mind. If you can answer this riddle, you're hired!

Three mothers and three daughters are reunited. What's the fewest number of people there can be?

Head to the panel number you believe is the correct answer. If you're wrackin' your brains but you still can't figure the answer, return to Page 7 to find another employer.

**48**

You have successfully completed your adventure! The members of the town council are pleased.

You've unlocked the Banditos Mission. This mission allows you to start a new game with new objectives: let chaos reign and kill everyone you encounter outside of Your Town. Each kill will be worth $100. Be careful not to kill people that play key roles in your adventure. You goal is to have a town with a maximum of 5 Safety points and $5000 in the bank in under 12 months. When you complete the Banditos Mission, make your way to 163.

Damn! You left the wanted poster in the sheriff's office. Will you be able to identify Goro-The-Fool from memory? Make your choice then bring him back in 82.

**51**

Footprints, recently made. Someone was here! You decide to keep one hand on your revolver, allowing you to fire twice during an attack.

Continue to 316.

**52**

You have no rights, I did nothing illegal! This is scandalous!

He's right. His trial is a fiasco like Your Town has never seen, costing you $800 in legal fees. In addition, the Casino shuts its doors for the next two months. You will not earn its income during that period. After noting this in your Ledger, return to your office in 88.

**53**

The poor soul is in shock, unaware of what just happened. This smelled like a trap from miles away, and you're certain you just avoided a quick death. Get out while you still can in 120.

**54**

Mister Mayor, we have a catastrophe on our hands! It seems that the snake oil salesman was a veritable charlatan! Since his arrival, there's been an epidemic of diarrhea in town and the residents of the neighboring town, South Valley, had the same problem when he visited there! If you have neither a doctor nor a Hospital, your population loses 10 residents. Regardless, your Approval rating drops 10 points and you must chase this trickster out of Your Town. You will no longer gain $100 per month from the stall. Furthermore, if the fraud is named Roger Kouzak, your citizens demand that you reimburse them for the tar and feathers used to punish him. This costs you a handsome $150.

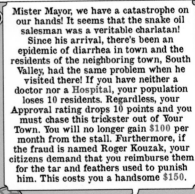

After removing the Snake Oil Stall from your map and its income from your Ledger, return to 88. Of course, you will not be able to visit the Engineer until another month has passed.

051-052-053-054

**55** Not bad, son! You've got potential. There's certainly something we can make of you. Come to my office in 257.

**56** Well, I'll have you know that I raise goats. I have a large farm a few miles that way. But I'd be lying if I said I weren't getting a wee bit bored. Not a soul around, except for old Herbert.

If you wish to invite him to join Your Town, go to 75. To make him an offer to buy his land, go to 303. If you'd rather end this discussion, go to 336.

**57** Hmm. I'll... I'll think about it. Now, please go, I have work to do.

It would appear you found the words to convince him. Your relationship with the sheriff improves one rank (note this in your Ledger). You can now return to your office in 88.

**58** How goes it, son? What're you doin' 'round these parts?

If you wish to make him an offer for his mine, go to 158. If you wish to know who owns these lands, go to 8. If you wish to ask him what he'd like the mayor of Your Town to do for him, go to 275. If you're not interested in any of the above, wave goodbye to the old man and continue in 333.

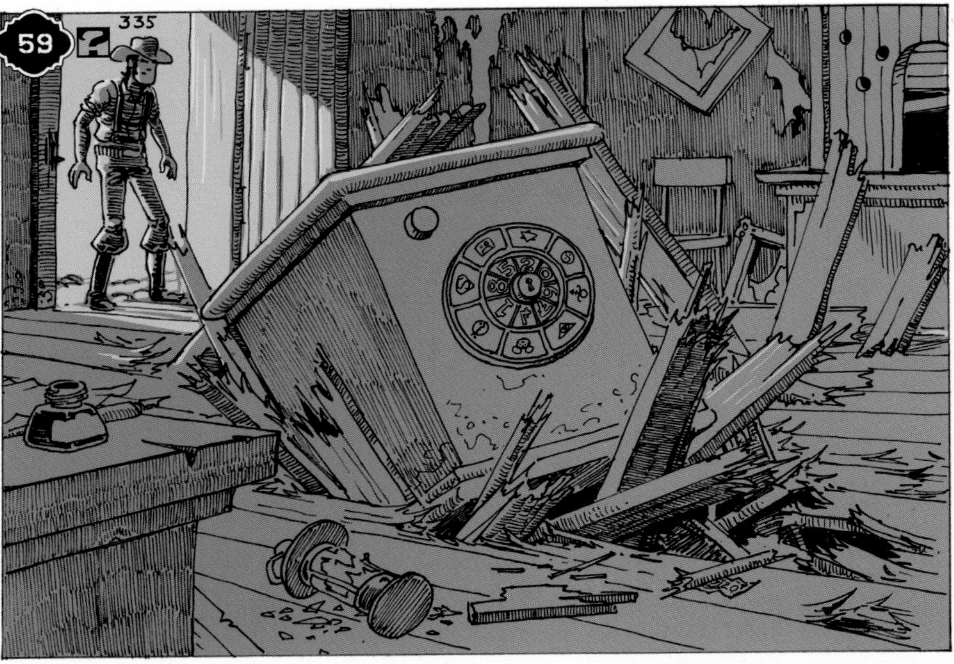
59
335

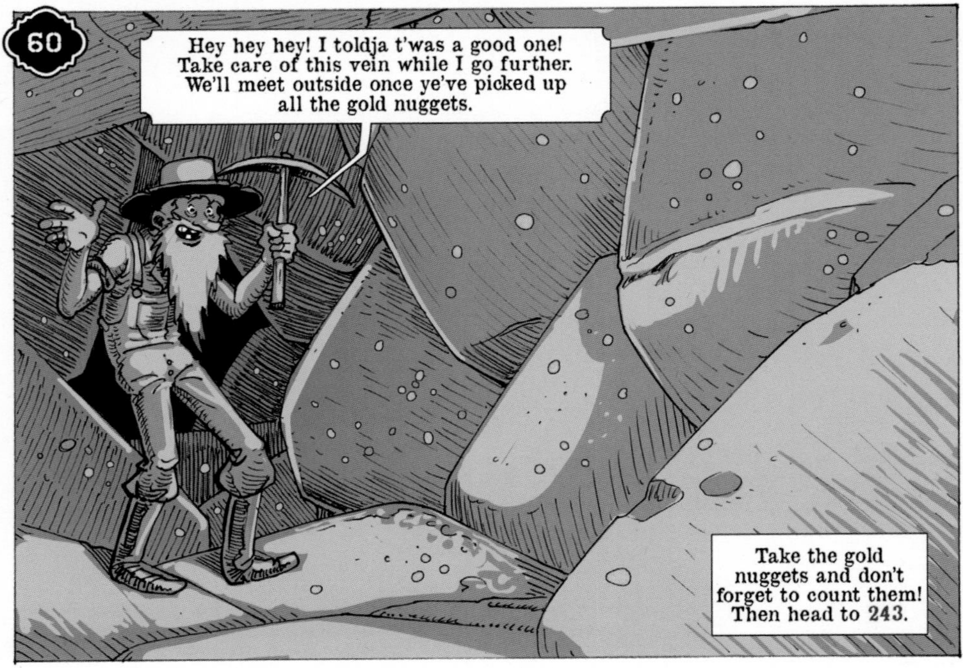
60
Hey hey hey! I toldja t'was a good one! Take care of this vein while I go further. We'll meet outside once ye've picked up all the gold nuggets.
Take the gold nuggets and don't forget to count them! Then head to 243.

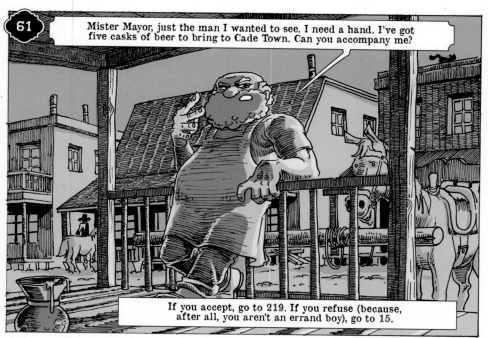

**61** Mister Mayor, just the man I wanted to see. I need a hand. I've got five casks of beer to bring to Cade Town. Can you accompany me?

If you accept, go to 219. If you refuse (because, after all, you aren't an errand boy), go to 15.

**62** Not much is happenin' 'round these parts. You can turn back and return to your office in 88, or continue under the blazing sun in 319.

**63**

After reaping the benefits of your status as mayor, your career comes to an end, as you failed to convince the town of your value. I strongly encourage you to review your methods before starting a new game.

**64**

I've got a letter for a certain Mauricette. Do you know her?

Of course I know her, she's my daughter. I'll be happy to give it to her.

Huzzah! Now there's a successful mission! You leave the town in 262.

This crazy fool probably hoped to protect his treasure. Will you find it one day? You can go back to Your Town in 88.

Attacking them was neither your best nor brightest idea, was it? I'm afraid your adventure comes to an end here.

THE END

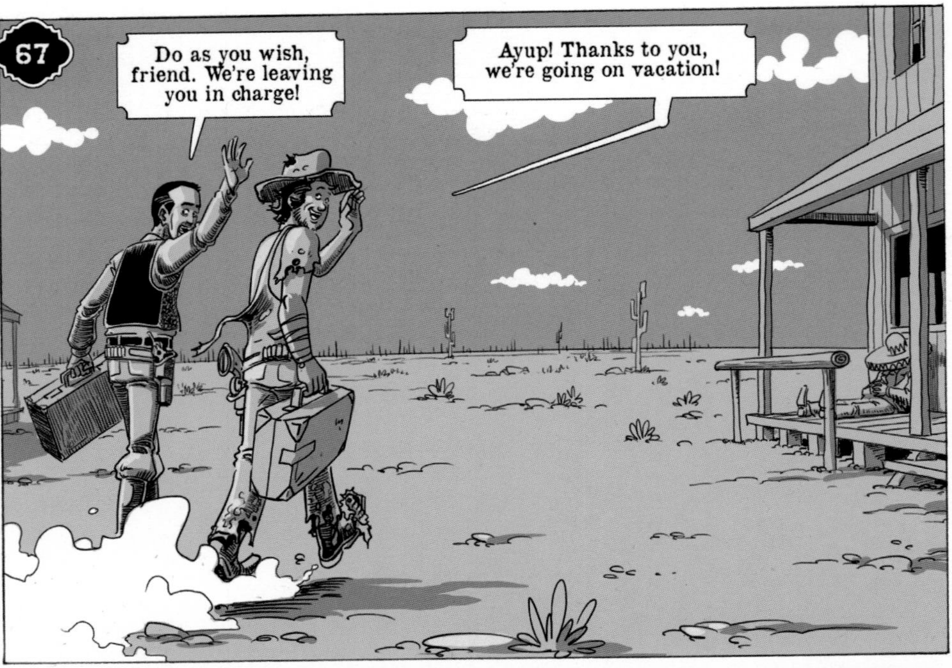
67
Do as you wish, friend. We're leaving you in charge!
Ayup! Thanks to you, we're going on vacation!

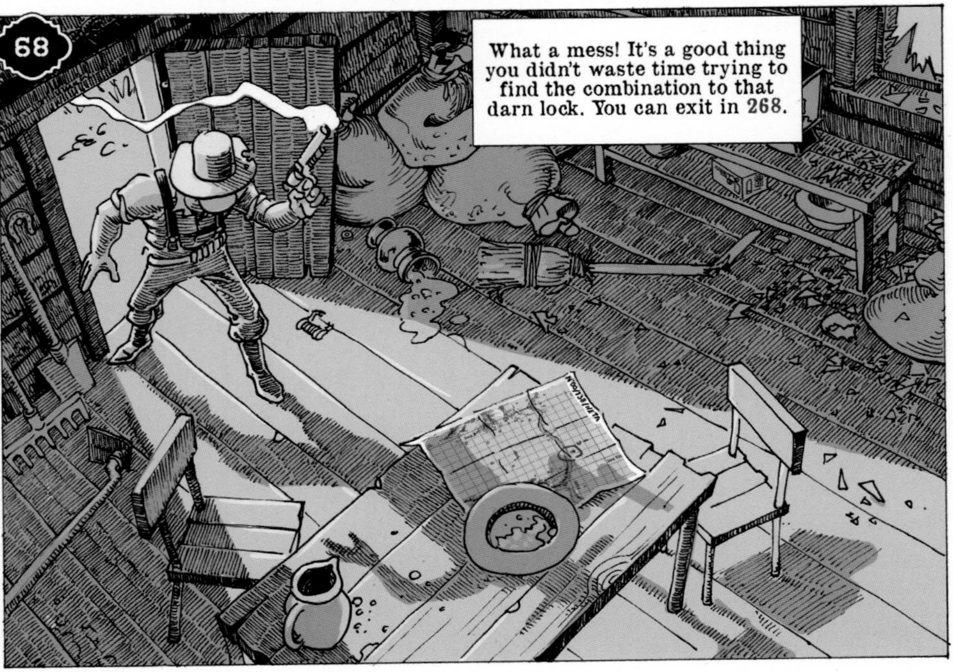
68
What a mess! It's a good thing you didn't waste time trying to find the combination to that darn lock. You can exit in 268.

These chaps are clearly not interested in conversation. Your response depends on how many bullets you have. To fire, hold your pencil approximately 6 inches from the panel and drop it on the two shooters. If you hit your enemies, you win. In that case, go to 265. Otherwise, head to 176.

Well done, cowboy! For $150 you've just acquired a nice location and a few planks to build your Small House. Add it to the Map found at the end of this book (it takes up 1 square). Next, add 1 population in your Ledger (since you're now officially a resident of the town) and $50 to your monthly income. Then, return to the saloon in 80. If this is your first building and you would like to learn more about how to build them, go to 339.

You've just found a hidden treasure!
Note it in your Ledger and go back to 59.

**73**

Ha ha! I belong in the wild, my boy! I don't give two hoots about the city, and you should have guessed as much seeing as how I'm readin' this 3-year old newspaper.

He's not going to follow you, no matter how much you argue. However, you can ask him if he's got anything to sell in 249, or leave his house in 120.

**74**

What a welcome! I did not expect to meet you so soon Mister Mayor. May I speak with you privately?

Clearly, this lady wanted to meet you. You can invite her to join you in your office in 313, or let her know that, sadly, you are too busy and go back to 88.

**75**

Good lord, why not? I could move my goats too. All right. I'm moving!

Good job! You now have a new resident. In addition, he moves in with his herd of goats and his tools, everything needed to build a Big Farm. You need only tell him where to build it (this construction won't cost you anything). You can continue in 336 or return to Your Town in 88.

**76**

I understand that you are very busy Mister Mayor, but the reputation of our Post Office will be terribly harmed!

The engineer was right: word of this lost letter spread quickly. The citizens are boycotting the Post Office, which will not generate any income for the next 3 months. After noting all this, go back to 88. As you know, you will not be able to visit the engineer again until the end of next month.

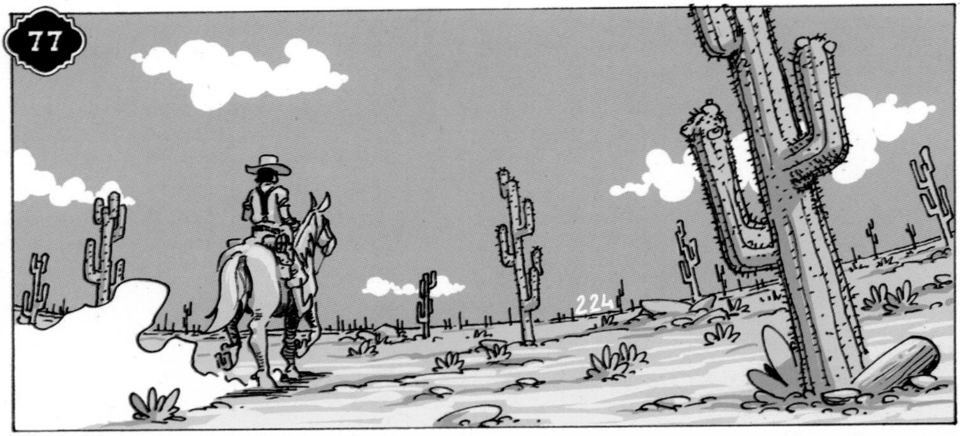
77
224

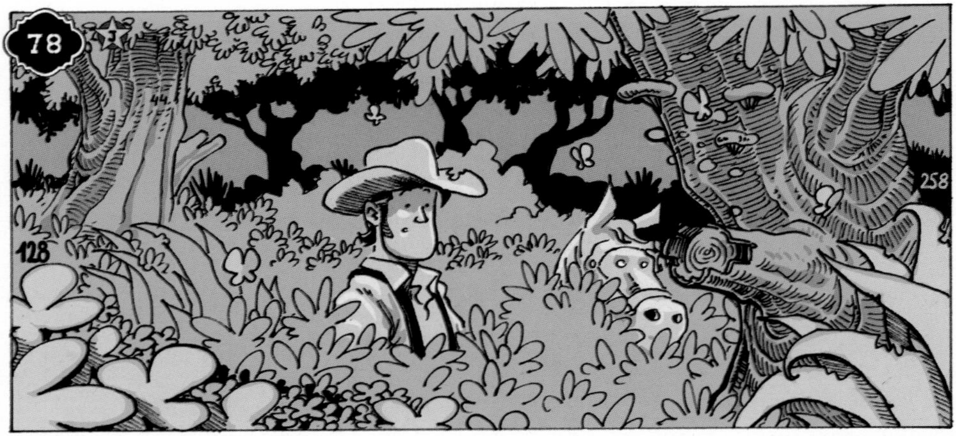
78
128
258

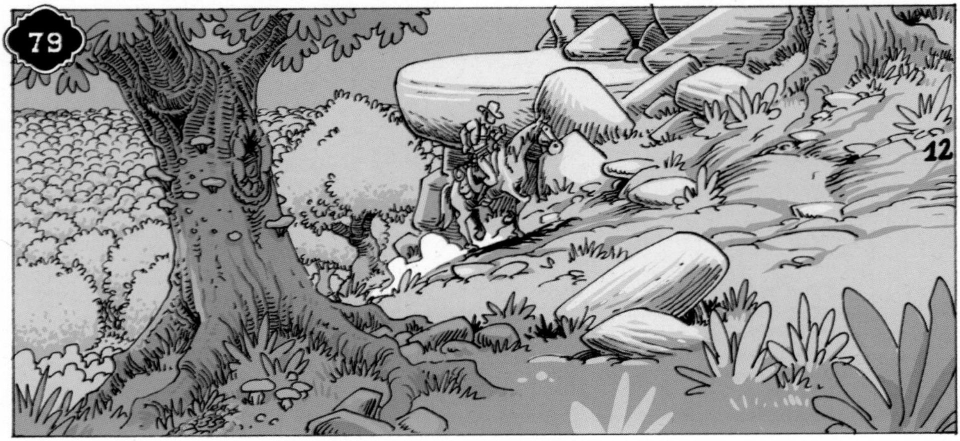
79
12

So, I hear yer settling in?

Yup!

What's possessed you kid, settling in this dung heap? There's no one around, even less to do, nothin' worth nothin'. The last time anything exciting happened was when that fool Jackman, hammered a nail in his toe while building this 'ere saloon.

Precisely! I've got grand plans for this town, and I think that within a year, it'll be one of the finest in the west.

Hold on... did I hear you right? Did you just proclaim yerself mayor of this town?

No no no, sheriff! I already have Jackman, the engineer, the undertaker, and old McKenzie's approval. I'm only missing yours.

If you failed the shooting test or haven't worked with the sheriff yet, go to 206. Otherwise, go to 195.

**81**

This was self-defense. Don't feel guilty. Old Catingan was completely crazy. Go to 65 to search him.

**82**

Is that a 'P' I see stenciled on his hat?

If the answer is yes, go to 31. If the answer is no, go to 13.

**83**

Your courage and heroic act increase your Approval by 3 points. Go back to 88.

**84**

Yours for only $500! It lets ya to fire twice as fast as that thing you got hangin' on yer belt...

You can decline the man's offer and return to 202. If you do choose to purchase this weapon, it allows you to fire twice as many shots as you're allowed. Once the transaction completed and noted in your Ledger, go to 202.

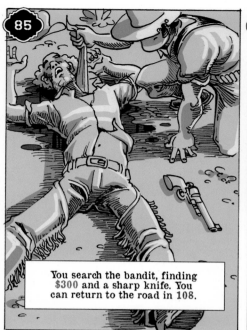

85

You search the bandit, finding $300 and a sharp knife. You can return to the road in 108.

86

What're you doin' here, stranger?

To inform him that you are the new mayor of Your Town, go to 91. If you don't feel like answering him, ignore him and continue on your way to 112. If you are looking for Lady Rekina, go to 298. If you get the feeling that this man is slightly irritated and you'd rather not upset him, turn around and head back to your office in 88.

87

19

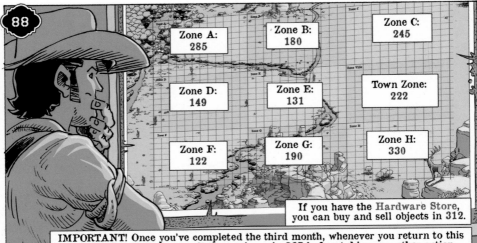

**88**

| | | |
|---|---|---|
| Zone A: 285 | Zone B: 180 | Zone C: 245 |
| Zone D: 149 | Zone E: 131 | Town Zone: 222 |
| Zone F: 122 | Zone G: 190 | Zone H: 330 |

If you have the Hardware Store, you can buy and sell objects in 312.

IMPORTANT! Once you've completed the third month, whenever you return to this panel you must first consult the engineer in 267 before taking any other action.

If you've just returned from exploring, a month has passed. Note this in your Ledger and update your Bank Account with your monthly income. Then, you can explore new zones in order to find raw resources, meet new folks, and (in time) buy new land. If (and only if) you've just returned from exploring, you can visit the streets of Your Town in 222. Note that you can ONLY do this **up to 5 times** during your adventure (keep track in your Ledger). If you've just completed the twelfth month of your adventure, go to 204.

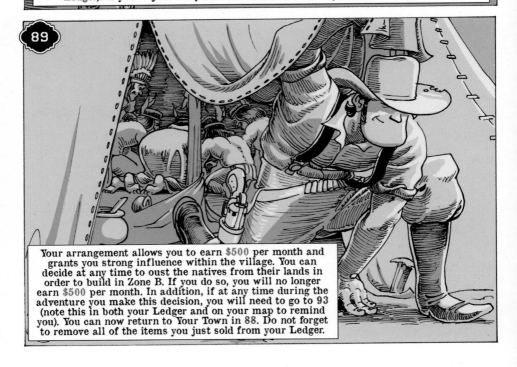

**89**

Your arrangement allows you to earn $500 per month and grants you strong influence within the village. You can decide at any time to oust the natives from their lands in order to build in Zone B. If you do so, you will no longer earn $500 per month. In addition, if at any time during the adventure you make this decision, you will need to go to 93 (note this in both your Ledger and on your map to remind you). You can now return to Your Town in 88. Do not forget to remove all of the items you just sold from your Ledger.

You may take the letter with you. Then, return to 95.

The sheriff invites you to follow him to panel 326.

**93**

You've just made the worst decision of your career. The citizens, who all profoundly respected the natives, are enraged. Furious, 20 residents leave your town. In addition, the natives have sworn to take revenge. Because of this, Safety drops by 10 points.

After noting all of these changes, you make your way to 253 to begin your new building projects.

**94**

Fredo Maxwell? Never heard of him. Sorry.

You can enter the **Casino** in 252.

**95**

If you have a rope, you can improvise a grappling hook to catch the letter found next to the skeleton. Then, head to 90 to read it.

After quenching your thirst, you can slowly get back on the road in 280.

You offer to...

Give them $1500 (if you have it): go to 272

Give each of them a job: go to 113

Limit construction to 5 buildings so as not to crowd them; go to 143

Build a house for each of them and count them as part of your population; go to 113

Trade their territory for another one; go to 143

Give them a Mine (if you have one); go to 272

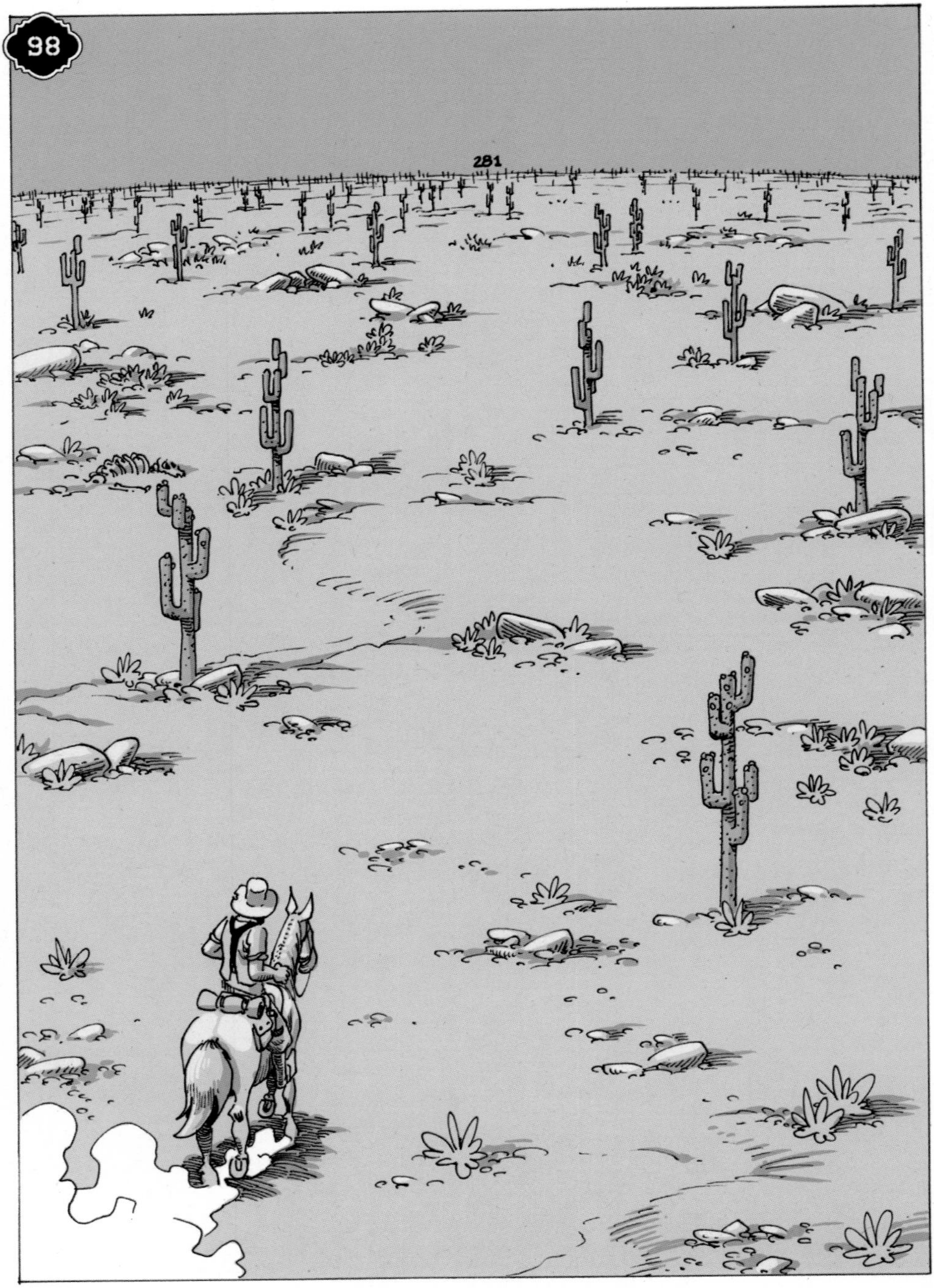
98
281

**99** Oh really? You think business will pick up again? Well this lifts my spirit. Thank you Mister Mayor.

At least someone's happy. Return to 88.

**100** The next day...

I never thought you'd find it. Bravo, son! Bravo.

Almost there!

**101**

# THE DAILY BUGLE

## OLD BARRY'S DEATH

It is a sad day in Fonbellon. Indeed, good old Barry, the distinguished barman and owner of the only saloon several miles around has just left us. In a very sad accident, the poor man was crushed under his freshly repainted signboard as he was trying to hang it back up. Many of Fonbellon's residents, shocked and saddened by the news, have indicated that they would soon leave Fonbellon.

### AT LAST!

A treaty has just been signed between the natives and the residents of the area to ensure that peace would be sustained. Article continued on page 2.

### ROBBERY

A very expensive brooch ($1000) was stolen in a holdup committed by the infamous desperados Paoli and Medina. It has been said that they found refuge in Brasco county. Article continued on page 4.

You can return to 95.

**A**

If you have a Train Station, a judge and a teacher have just arrived in Your Town. They both count as esteemed residents.

Return to your previous panel.

**B**

If your Approval rating is more than 25 points, a new esteemed resident has just arrived.

Return to your previous panel.

**C**

If you have more than 300 wood in stock, the cost of your next building is halved.

Return to your previous panel.

**D**

If you have more Jobs than Population, you attract 10 new residents who will immediatly build a Big House at no cost to you.

Return to your previous panel.

**E**

If you have a Bank, but you do NOT have a Reinforced Steel Vault, the Bank is robbed. You lose $1000.

Return to your previous panel.

**F**

If you have more Population than Jobs, each building earns you half as much money as planned until this trend is reversed.

Return to your previous panel.

**G**

If you have buildings next to water, you lose 3 points of your choice (Approval Safety, Health, Education or a combination) because of a flood.

Return to your previous panel.

**H**

If you have a good relationship with a doctor, he decides to invest $500 in Your Town's future.

Return to your previous panel.

**I**

If you built a Prison close to a House (either 2 or 1 squares away), your Approval rating drops 10 points.

Return to your previous panel.

**J**

If you have a Snake Oil Stall, its latest concoction leads to an epidemic of strong diarrhea. Your Approval rating drops 5 points.

Return to your previous panel.

**K**

If you have more Food than Population, each surplus Food point earns you $10.

Return to your previous panel.

**L**

If your Safety rating is below 15, your town is attacked by a gang of outlaws. You lose $500 and 5 Approval points.

Return to your previous panel.

**M**

If your Education rating is 10 or higher, the state grants you $1000.

Return to your previous panel.

**N**

If your Health rating is 7 or higher, a new doctor moves into town. He counts as an esteemed resident.

Return to your previous panel.

**O**

If you have killed 3 or more men during your adventure, your Safety rating goes up 5 points.

Return to your previous panel.

**P**

If you own a Mine, a new vein was just discovered. You gain $1000.

Return to your previous panel.

**Q**

A tax collector has just arrived in town and requires 10% of your Bank Account (to know how much to give him, divide your money in the bank by 10).

Return to your previous panel.

**R**

If you have at least 4 Farms adjacent to one another, a rat swarm invades and destroys part of your harvest. You lose 10 Food points.

Return to your previous panel.

**S**

If you have a Blacksmith, a fire destroys it along with all adjacent buildings.

Return to your previous panel.

**T**

If you have a Train Station, the train has just derailed. Luckily, nobody was hurt, but you will need to spend $500 in repairs.

Return to your previous panel.

**U**

If you own buildings that share a border with water, your Approval goes up 1 point for each of those buildings.

Return to your previous panel.

**V**

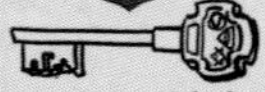

If you have this key, two bandits attack you. You manage to lose them, but in the process you also lose $150.

Return to your previous panel.

**W**

If you have a Hardware Store, the clerk rewards you for your recent acquisition with a box containing 10 bullets.

Return to your previous panel.

**X**

If you entered a pact with the natives in which you promised not to kill any animals, and you have broken this pact, all of your buildings in Zone B are destroyed. Lose all benefits for those buildings. Return to your previous panel.

**Y**

If you've built anything in Zone A, the people who live here are terrified of evil spirits that roam the streets at night. You lose 10 residents and 10 Approval points. Return to your previous panel.

You can download this sheet for easier reference at www. vanrydergames.com.

**103** You aren't makin' fun of me, are ya?

The prospector seems to have an axe to grind with you, and your relationship drops one level (make a note of this in your Ledger). You decide to return to town on Page 7 to find another job.

**104**

**105** Mister Mayor, another disaster! This letter became stuck in the bottom of one of our mailbags and was never sent. As a result, the reputation of our Post Office is at stake. We should absolutely deliver it as soon as possible. Will you handle it?

If you'll deliver the letter, leave immediately to South Valley in 202. You can also refuse and go to 76.

**106**

You barely grazed it, but that was enough to scare it away. Nice work! Go to 221 or 46.

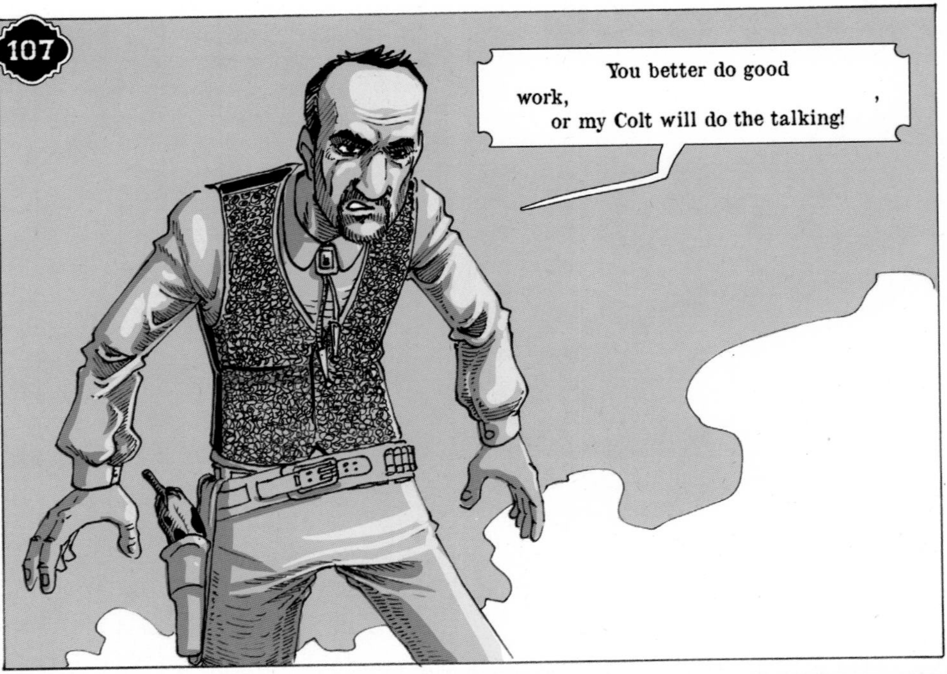
107
You better do good
work, ,
or my Colt will do the talking!

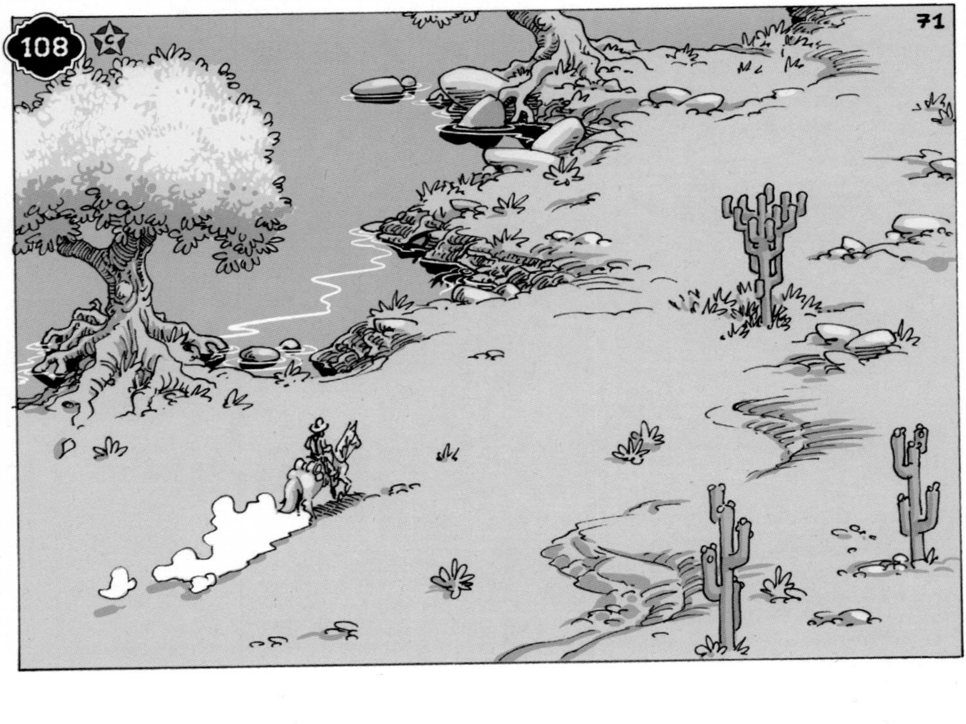
108
71

After shedding a few tears, Lady Rekina invites you to follow her in **299**.

You've just gotten your hands on a hidden treasure that earns you **$1000**! Isn't life wonderful? Note it in your Ledger and then return to where you came from.

**111**

Go meet the fellow in 320. Otherwise, let him continue on his way and head to 336.

**112**

Oooooffff! The sheriff lassos you and yanks you off your horse. Go to 173.

**113**

We are not interested. Leave now, before the fury of our people tramples you like a mighty herd of buffalo!

The chieftain insists you never return to their lands (Zone B). You can return to your office in 88.

**114**

Mister Mayor, we should head to the Casino post haste! A man named Fredo Maxwell is on a winning streak at the tables!

If you wish to go to the Casino, head to 133. If you prefer to let everything work itself out, head to 32.

**115**

If your relationship with old McKenzie is bad (B) or you simply do not wish to talk to him, go to 333. Otherwise, you can speak with him in 58.

**116**

You've discovered a gold vein. If you build a Gold Mine here, it will be worth $500 per month. Return to your office in 88.

**117**

BLAM!!!

Geez, they weren't kidding! You can hide behind barrels in 148 or get the hell out of Dodge in 88.

**118**

Thank you, sir!

After pocketing the $300 and noting it in your Ledger, you head to the saloon in 282.

119

What an impressive beast! If you own a long-range rifle, you slaughter this bear in one shot in 233. If, however, you want to attempt to kill it with a revolver, go to 196... but don't you say you haven't been warned.
If you do not have a rifle or simply wish to spare this animal's life, you quietly leave the area and return to town in 88.

120

87

A rather embarrassing situation. However, you can take the hunter's long-range rifle and 3 bullets. Note them in your Ledger. You discreetly return to 146.

115

**123**

You've finally found the means to cross the river and can now explore this new land. Keep an eye out, as you wouldn't want to come face to face with a puma. At any time, if you think you've fully explored this zone, you can head to 278.

**124**

You can continue heading towards the smoke trail by going to 250. Or turn back in 49.

**125**

Heh heh! I've got you now, don't I? This mine ain't worth squat since you helped me git all the gold out of it.

Rascally old man! You go to 58 after "missing out" on the deal of the century.

**126**

By Jove, we can purchase this land in Zone G for $500.

The choice is yours. After deciding, head back to 88.

**127**

You come at a good time, Mister Mayor. I'm unemployed and I'd like to build a Carpenter's Shop. Can you help me?

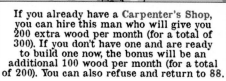

If you already have a Carpenter's Shop, you can hire this man who will give you 200 extra wood per month (for a total of 300). If you don't have one and are ready to build one now, the bonus will be an additional 100 wood per month (for a total of 200). You can also refuse and return to 88.

**128**

**129**

You can continue in 38 or, weary, you can return to Your Town in 88.

**130** 256

**131** 36

A beautiful land where you could build as far as the eye can see. But be warned, the crushing heat and lack of water will force you to find solutions to ensure this project is successful. With this in mind, each building will cost you an extra $100. So, will you build here (Zone D)? These lands are free. After making your decision, you can return to 88.

You can attempt to find the combination. You also have the option of using your revolver (if you have one). In that case, lose one bullet and go to 68.
If you choose to do nothing, return to 146.

**135**

Come in, come in! Don't be scared. In fact, you'll help me out in 291.

**136**

Native burial grounds... better not stay here for too long. And forget about building on these lands. The natives would consider this an act of provocation. You can return to 78.

**137**

A wise decision, Mister Mayor.

Your Approval rating goes up 2 points, but you lose $500. Now head back to 88.

**138**

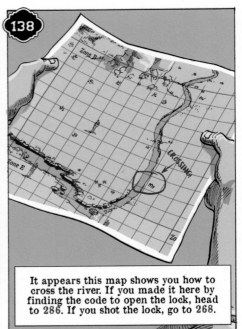

It appears this map shows you how to cross the river. If you made it here by finding the code to open the lock, head to 286. If you shot the lock, go to 268.

**139**

Are you helping or daydreaming?

After helping Norman the undertaker, go to 118.

**140**

If you have a water bottle, you can fill it up. Otherwise, have a good drink before returning to 256.

**141**

If you shot all four men, go to 289.

If you shot one or more of these bandits (A, B, or D) go to 155.

If you ONLY shot C, go to 207.

**142**

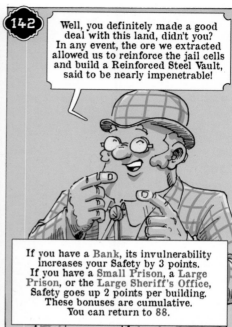

Well, you definitely made a good deal with this land, didn't you? In any event, the ore we extracted allowed us to reinforce the jail cells and build a Reinforced Steel Vault, said to be nearly impenetrable!

If you have a Bank, its invulnerability increases your Safety by 3 points. If you have a Small Prison, a Large Prison, or the Large Sheriff's Office, Safety goes up 2 points per building. These bonuses are cumulative. You can return to 88.

**143**

Now, this sounds interesting. Give me $1000 and a plot of land, and you will be able to build on our territory, but no more than 5 buildings.

He drives a hard bargain. Note that you can only offer a plot of land on which nothing has been built. If you do not have one, you cannot close this deal. If you accept his offer, go to 253. Otherwise, return to Your Town in 88.

**144**

**145**

You're clearly not welcome here. What will you do? You can advance with your weapon drawn and confront the natives directly in **247**. You can also raise your hands to show that you're coming in peace in **295**. Or you can turn around and head back to your office in **88**. In this case, you will neither be able to return to or build in Zone B, even if you purchased it.

**146**

You can also choose to head back to 38.

**147** I see you've acquired some land since last time. Impressive! But did you know that this area, in Zone C, belongs to me? I shall make you a deal: if you're willing to split evenly all income you receive from the buildings you build in this zone, I will let you have it for $500. What do you say?

After making your decision, you can explore Zone C in 77. If you have already visited it, immediately make your choice and go back to your office in 88. Don't forget that you will not be able to visit the engineer until another month has passed. **IMPORTANT!** Make sure to note in your Ledger that all buildings you construct in that zone will only earn you half of their income each month.

**148**

Staying hidden will make defending yourself difficult. You can raise your head in 225, tie a handkerchief to the gun barrel and use it as a white flag in 34, or turn tail and flee to your office in 88.

**149**

Mister Mayor, I've heard a lot about Your Town, and especially about your... how do you say it?

Skyscraper.

How charming!

Be that as it may, my city has need of your services. I'm ready and willing to give you anything you want for you to join us.

And, as proof of my sincerity, I travelled here in person, for many days, to meet you face to face.

And what's your city's name?

New York!

FIN

**151**

It's a safe bet to say that this man had bad intentions. Thanks to your intervention, Safety and Approval go up 5 points each. In addition, you earn $500 by reselling what he was carrying. You can now return to 88.

**152**

Mister mayor, we have a slight problem with a resident in Zone H. Herbert, the old man who's been living in the forest for many decades, is fed up with all the comings and goings as well as the construction around his small shack. He demands $500 to leave the area and build a house elsewhere.

If you accept, go to 137.
Go to 324, if you refuse.

**153**

We have a problem, Mister Mayor. While the Train Station was essential to our town's growth, it has attracted some unwanted attention. Indeed, safety is at risk and we have lost 3 Safety points because of this.

If you have a Large Sheriff's Office or an Army Fort in Your Town, go to 214. Otherwise, go to 208.

**154**

This river will be difficult to cross. You can try crossing in 174, follow it in 104, or return to Your Town in 88.

**155** ⭐ Q

Thanks, cowboy! Without you, I would've been done for sure!

Your accuracy still needs work, and the bandits managed to escape, but even so, you've saved this man's life.

Take this key, my friend. It's the cause of all my troubles, but it could make you rich. It opens a safe located in the ghost town of Fontbellon, north east of here. I don't know what's inside that safe. But one thing's for certain, this key is coveted by many, so be on your guard.

Make your way to 251.

**156**

No one has EVER spoken to me this way! This is outrageous! Well, let's see how you handle your town without a sheriff, gimcrack mayor!

Oh shucks. Slightly annoyed by your attitude, the sheriff was close to leaving. Lucky for you, his sense of duty makes him stay. But your relationship with him is ruined forever. You will no longer be able to improve it, even if given that option later in your adventure. Note your relationship is bad (B) in your Ledger. You may now return to your office in 88.

**157**

If you have a knife or a hook, you can pick the lock and go to 269. You can also shoot the lock by going to 293. Otherwise, head back to 335.

**158**

Why...yes... I could sell it to ya. It's almost exhausted anyway...

$800 and it's yours. In'erested?

If you have $800 and you find the offer acceptable, make your way to the mine in 297. If you have a good (G) relationship with McKenzie, go to 125 before finalizing the transaction. If you are not interested, or do not have enough money, continue on your way in 333. You will be able to return here (note the panel number).

**159**

You find yourself with many options: turn back and return to 49, shoot one or more of these men in 141 (note the matching letters), or peacefully go to meet them in 69.

You were able to impress everyone with your planning and project management skills. The town trusts you blindly, allowing you go even bigger. You've just unlocked the special authorization to build a Skyscraper. However, you must first accumulate $5000. You have three months to complete this mission. Go to 88 now. Of course, you can only go to places you haven't previously explored. If you complete your mission in under three months, go to 150. Otherwise, your adventure will end there.

They arrive in the nick of time and help you to claim the land within Zone B. On the other hand, we can't say this was a glorious victory: your Approval rating drops 20 points. If you have a Grocery Store, it's owner, a native, shuts the doors and leaves Your Town. You lose 1 population, the Grocery Store, and all of its advantages (bonuses, income, job, and approval). You can now return to 88.

**163** You've managed to instill terror all over Your Town... and beyond!

The death toll is in the double digits...

..which makes some folks very happy.

But can you let chaos rule without consequences?

THE END

**164**

WARNING
NATIVE TERRITORY
ALCOHOL IS
FORBIDDEN
309

If you have any alcohol, you can throw it away before continuing. Of course, if you're a little daring, you can choose to keep it...

**165**

Here is where you need to cross!

Thanks to this clue, you can leave the native lands and go to **144**. You can also return to Your Town in **88**.

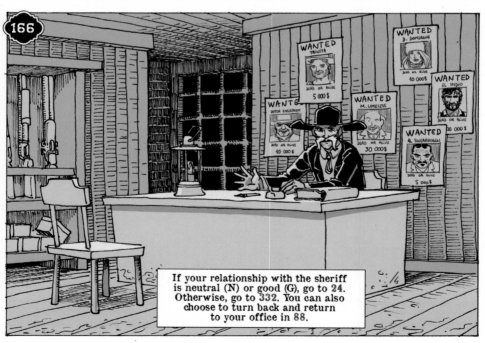

**166**

If your relationship with the sheriff is neutral (N) or good (G), go to **24**. Otherwise, go to **332**. You can also choose to turn back and return to your office in **88**.

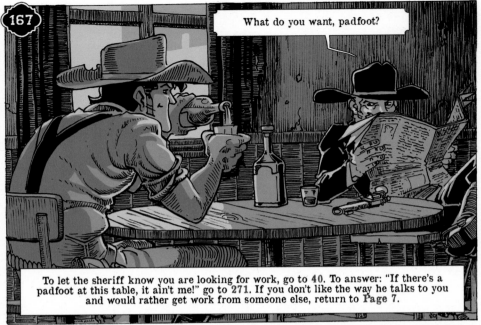

What do you want, padfoot?

To let the sheriff know you are looking for work, go to 40. To answer: "If there's a padfoot at this table, it ain't me!" go to 271. If you don't like the way he talks to you and would rather get work from someone else, return to Page 7.

If this path looks too risky, you can stop exploring and return to your office in 88.

**169**

You're right... it is rather simple. Too simple for me not to fill my pockets!

The rules are easy:

Each player gets 500 tokens. The ante is 100 tokens. The dealer deals each player one card.

The first player announces what his card is, either the truth or a lie, and bids a number of tokens of his choice.

The second player can either fold (choosing to believe that her opponent's card is higher than hers) or she can announce that her card is higher and bid as many tokens as she wants. Of course, a player can also bluff.

The first player will then end the round by bidding or folding. If he bids, the highest card wins. Bluffing is important, just as much as spotting it.

If you would rather not start this game, you can leave the Casino in 30. If you truly know what you're doing, the game starts in 191.

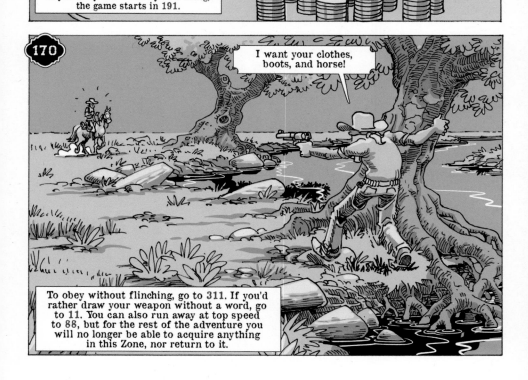

**170**

I want your clothes, boots, and horse!

To obey without flinching, go to 311. If you'd rather draw your weapon without a word, go to 11. You can also run away at top speed to 88, but for the rest of the adventure you will no longer be able to acquire anything in this Zone, nor return to it.

**171**

It was a good move to build this Cemetery, Mister Mayor. It's the most profilable location in town. This month only, due to the surge in desperados and coyote attacks, you beat all previous records: $500 extra! If you've welcomed a snake oil salesman in town, you earn a total of $600. If the snake oil salesman's name is Roger Kouzak, that total is $700. Finally, you have a good (G) relationship with Norman the undertaker. He donated $200 to the town to show his thanks.

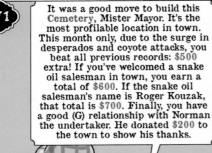

After noting down all of this, go back to 88. As you know, you won't be able to visit the engineer until another month has passed.

**172**

You can approach these riders discreetly in 159, holler to ask them to wait for you in 69, or turn back in 49.

**173**

Listen to me gringo... ...never set foot here again, ya hear me?

You've just ruined any chance of an alliance or business arrangement with Tanfaidey Town. After noting this in your Ledger, return to your office in 88. You will no longer be able to return to Zone F.

**174**

From the get-go this seemed like a mistake! You return to land in 104 without having crossed the river. If you own a rope, you limit the damage and only lose $500 (or all of your money if you have less than that). If you do not have a rope, in addition to losing that money, you also lose your weapon.

NOTE: If you find yourself in a combat situation, you will not be able to defend yourself until you've found or purchased a new revolver.

Not everyone is enthusiastic about your plans, but you do begin your term as mayor with an Approval rating of 5. During your adventure, you will meet residents satisfied with how you're managing the town, and others not so much. Each time this happens (satisfaction or disapproval), you must raise or lower your Approval rating.

This rating will have an impact on your adventure. If your citizens approve of your actions, you'll gain advantages. If your Approval rating gets too low, you risk being chased out of town before the end of your term. Now, head to 317.

Your assailants left you for dead. You owe your life to Your Town's doctor, who just happened to be traveling through the area. Return to 88 after staying in bed for a few days. Note that you will no longer be able to take the path towards Zone D. And sorry to inform you that, if you do not have a doctor in Your Town, you are dead and will need to restart your adventure.

Mmmkay... well I think there's more than just nuggets in there. But that's still good work you did. Here's $500 worth. Don't spend it all in one place now.

Note this reward under your Bank Account in your Ledger, then return to the saloon in 282.

To make him an offer to buy his land, go to 301. If you want to ask for help visiting Zone A, go to 201. If you wish to sell him alcohol or weapons (only possible if you have some on you), go to 89. You can also choose to leave the teepee and head back to town in 88.

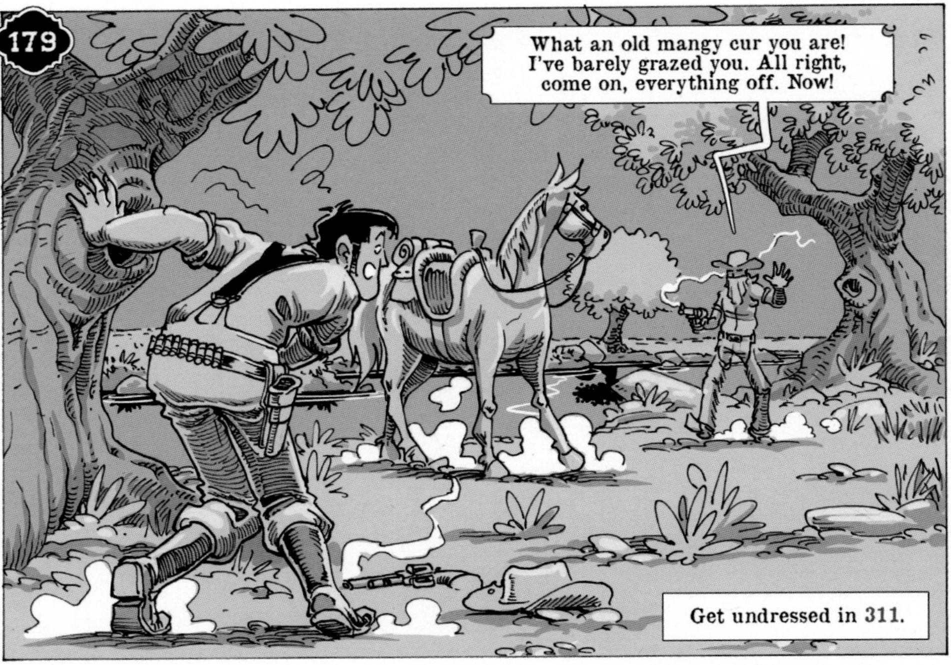
179
What an old mangy cur you are! I've barely grazed you. All right, come on, everything off. Now!
Get undressed in 311.

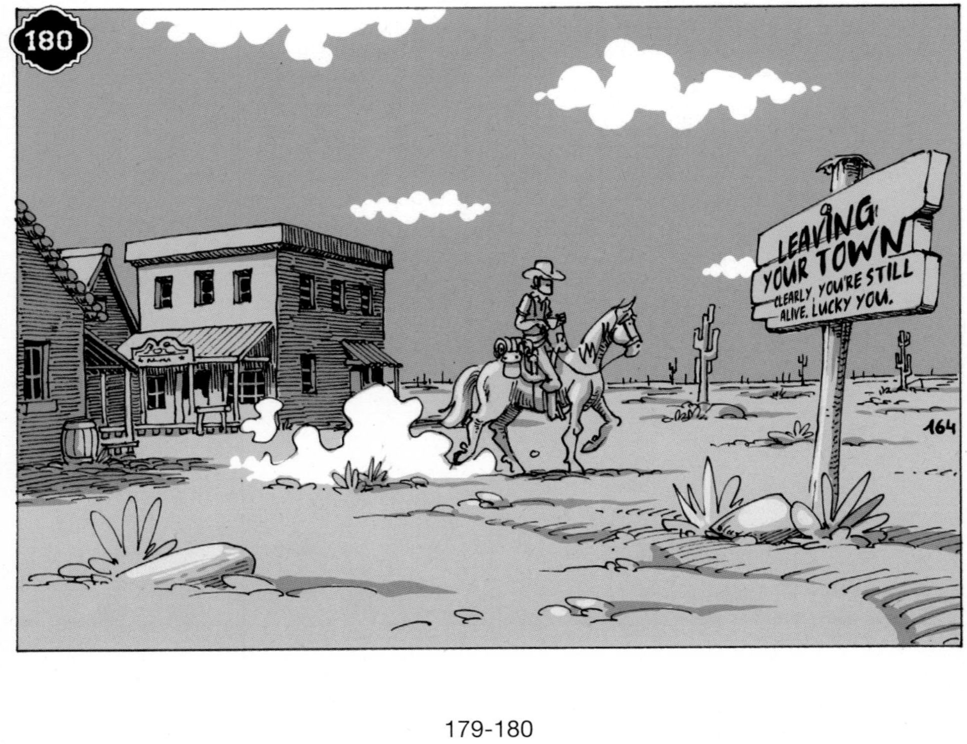
180
LEAVING YOUR TOWN
CLEARLY, YOU'RE STILL ALIVE. LUCKY YOU.

79

You've been on the road for days. Wouldn't it be prudent to head back to civilization in 88?

146

Your offer is interesting. Here's my proposal: if you have a Farmer's Market in your town, one of my merchants will come and sell their produce. In exchange, they will give you $50 per month. If you don't have a Farmer's Market, I offer to bring you enough food for 10 people each month, which will cost you $20.

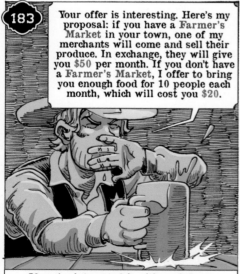

If you're interested in either of these offers, write it down in your Ledger (either a monthly profit of +$50, or +10 food and a monthly deduction of -$20). You can also refuse and return to 326.

I've never seen anyone scamper that fast!

You left in such a hurry that a few bills fell out of your bags. You lose $100 and return to your office in 88 to have a good cry.

A little tip: don't tell anyone about this misadventure...

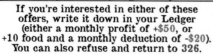

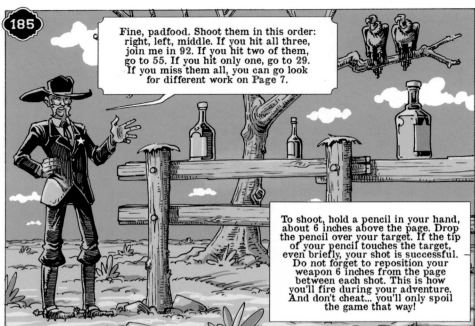

**185**

Fine, padfood. Shoot them in this order: right, left, middle. If you hit all three, join me in 92. If you hit two of them, go to 55. If you hit only one, go to 29. If you miss them all, you can go look for different work on Page 7.

To shoot, hold a pencil in your hand, about 6 inches above the page. Drop the pencil over your target. If the tip of your pencil touches the target, even briefly, your shot is successful. Do not forget to reposition your weapon 6 inches from the page between each shot. This is how you'll fire during your adventure. And don't cheat... you'll only spoil the game that way!

**186**

Having a good laugh at your expense, the desperados let you know that you've just killed an innocent man they were holding prisoner. Although they kindly made sure you were unharmed, they did free you of $500 and tie you to a rock. It's a few days before someone manages to free you. Go to 88, and don't forget to buy a new weapon (unless you owned more in addition to your revolver).

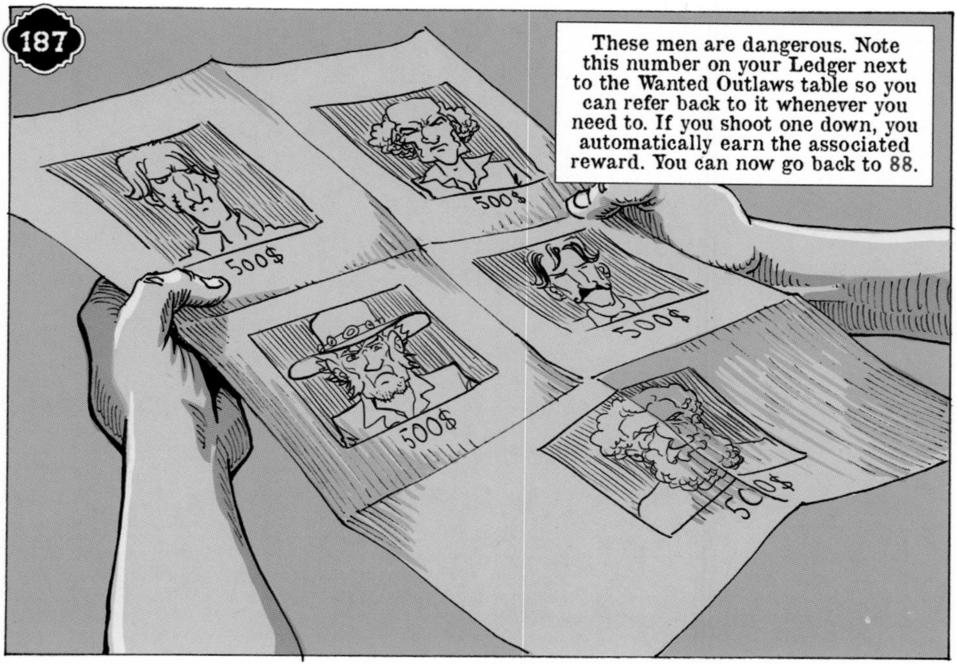
187
These men are dangerous. Note this number on your Ledger next to the Wanted Outlaws table so you can refer back to it whenever you need to. If you shoot one down, you automatically earn the associated reward. You can now go back to 88.
500$
500$
500$
500$
500$

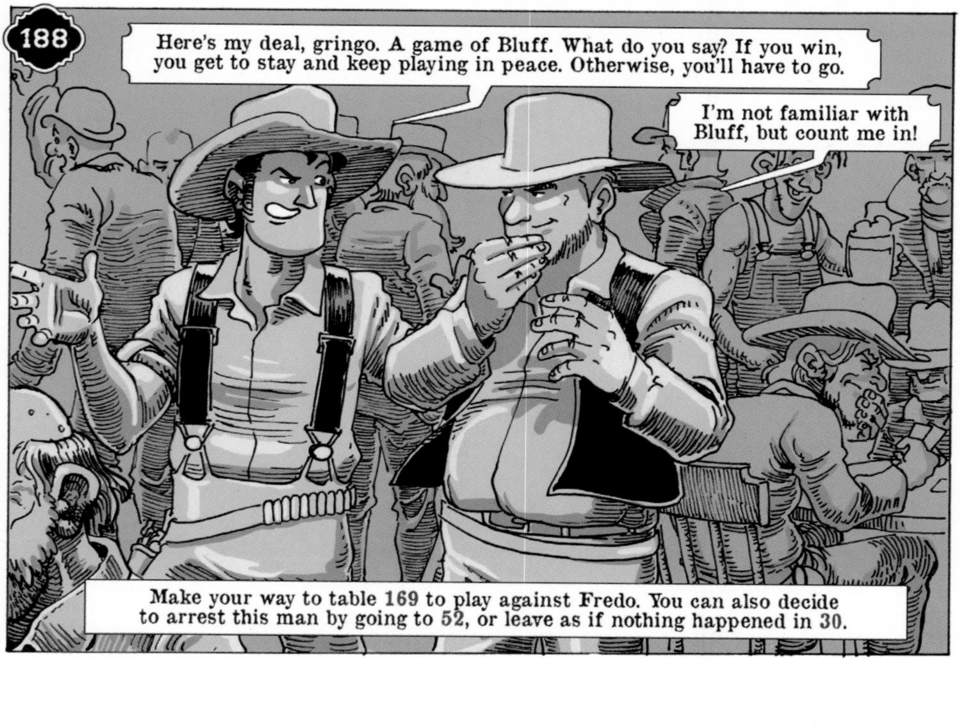
188
Here's my deal, gringo. A game of Bluff. What do you say? If you win, you get to stay and keep playing in peace. Otherwise, you'll have to go.
I'm not familiar with Bluff, but count me in!
Make your way to table 169 to play against Fredo. You can also decide to arrest this man by going to 52, or leave as if nothing happened in 30.

**189** If I'm satisfied? Well...

You gain 1 Approval point per building owned: School, Doctor's Office, Grocery Store, and Hospital. If you've built none of those buildings, you lose 3 Approval points. After adjusting your Ledger, return to 88.

**190**

**191** I got a jack and I bid 100 tokens.

You can fold in 266, or raise in 296 by bidding all of your tokens and bluffing that you have a queen.

**192**

**193**

No...business isn't going too well. If only there were a few outlaws robbing the eldery...but not even that. I'm afraid I'll soon need to close up shop.

If you have 10 or fewer Safety points, go to 99. Otherwise, head to 229.

**194**

My dear Mister Mayor, I regret to inform you that old Catingan was killed in cold-blood, most likely by an outlaw. In short, per his last will and testament, found not long ago, he bequeaths all of his land (Zone E) to Your Town.

From now on, Zone E belongs to you and you can build there. Return to your office in 88.

**195**

Well, well. You've certainly proven yourself, as well as managed to gain the population's approval. Hell, why not? But in a year, we'll do a review, and if we don't care for how you've handled the town, you'll leave. Agreed?

After agreeing to this, make your way to your office in 239.

**196**

If you hadn't been looking for trouble, this bear would have left you alone. But you just had to poke mother nature, and now you're dead. You may restart your adventure.

**197**

Blimey! I've gotta stop drinkin'... but I've given my word. I'll come ta work with you.

Sheriff Amilton joins your ranks and you gain 5 Safety points thanks to his experience. You can now return to 88.

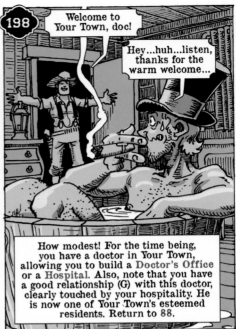

**198**

Welcome to Your Town, doc!

Hey...huh...listen, thanks for the warm welcome...

How modest! For the time being, you have a doctor in Your Town, allowing you to build a Doctor's Office or a Hospital. Also, note that you have a good relationship (G) with this doctor, clearly touched by your hospitality. He is now one of Your Town's esteemed residents. Return to 88.

**199**

With the minimum bid of 100 tokens, the game begins. And Mister Mayor wins the game.

Bravo! Thanks to you, Frédo and his team leave town. In addition, you impressed everyone with your poise. Your relationship with the sheriff improves by 1 level. You also gain 5 Safety and 5 Approval points. Return to 88.

**200**

HERE LIES THE MAYOR OF YOUR TOWN, WHOSE CAREER WAS SHORT-LIVED, BUT MEMORABLE. A PITY.

You can restart your adventure.

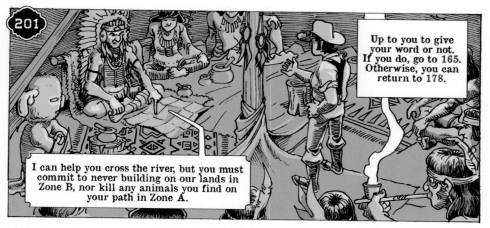

201

Up to you to give your word or not. If you do, go to 165. Otherwise, you can return to 178.

I can help you cross the river, but you must commit to never building on our lands in Zone B, nor kill any animals you find on your path in Zone A.

202

203

220

**204**

> Come in and sit down.
> Time for your review.

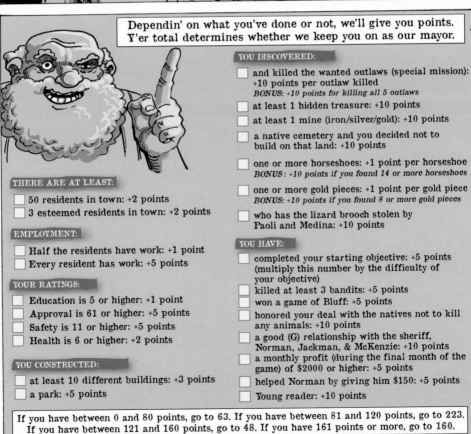

Dependin' on what you've done or not, we'll give you points. Y'er total determines whether we keep you on as our mayor.

**THERE ARE AT LEAST:**

- [ ] 50 residents in town: +2 points
- [ ] 3 esteemed residents in town: +2 points

**EMPLOYMENT:**

- [ ] Half the residents have work: +1 point
- [ ] Every resident has work: +5 points

**YOUR RATINGS:**

- [ ] Education is 5 or higher: +1 point
- [ ] Approval is 61 or higher: +5 points
- [ ] Safety is 11 or higher: +5 points
- [ ] Health is 6 or higher: +2 points

**YOU CONSTRUCTED:**

- [ ] at least 10 different buildings: +3 points
- [ ] a park: +5 points

**YOU DISCOVERED:**

- [ ] and killed the wanted outlaws (special mission): +10 points per outlaw killed
  *BONUS: +10 points for killing all 5 outlaws*
- [ ] at least 1 hidden treasure: +10 points
- [ ] at least 1 mine (iron/silver/gold): +10 points
- [ ] a native cemetery and you decided not to build on that land: +10 points
- [ ] one or more horseshoes: +1 point per horseshoe
  *BONUS: +10 points if you found 14 or more horseshoes*
- [ ] one or more gold pieces: +1 point per gold piece
  *BONUS: +10 points if you found 8 or more gold pieces*
- [ ] who has the lizard brooch stolen by Paoli and Medina: +10 points

**YOU HAVE:**

- [ ] completed your starting objective: +5 points (multiply this number by the difficulty of your objective)
- [ ] killed at least 3 bandits: +5 points
- [ ] won a game of Bluff: +5 points
- [ ] honored your deal with the natives not to kill any animals: +10 points
- [ ] a good (G) relationship with the sheriff, Norman, Jackman, & McKenzie: +10 points
- [ ] a monthly profit (during the final month of the game) of $2000 or higher: +5 points
- [ ] helped Norman by giving him $150: +5 points
- [ ] Young reader: +10 points

If you have between 0 and 80 points, go to 63. If you have between 81 and 120 points, go to 223. If you have between 121 and 160 points, go to 48. If you have 161 points or more, go to 160.

**205**

That's no way to enter someone's house, cowboy!

And he's right! Here you are, dead as doornail. You can restart your adventure.

**206**

What? You'll never get my support, stranger! Never!

The sheriff does not appear to approve of your plans, nor does he like you. Your relationship with him is now bad (B). Note this in your Ledger, then head to your office in 175.

**207**

Well, you're in a bad position, aren't ya? Make your way to 186.

**208**

Because of this, people are staying away from Your Town, which explains our current deficit. The income from the station has dropped to $150 per month and I'm afraid the situation will not change until our city is safer.

Unless you've built the **Large Sheriff's Office** or the **Army Fort**, the Train Station's income has been reduced to $150. You will be able to earn the full $400 once your Safety rating is at least 20 points. Go back to 88.

**209**

Your inscription was so bad that your first decision in this adventure is to shoot the author in cold blood. You can now begin to play in earnest on page 1.

**210**

I saved you a spot. I have no doubts that you'll be visiting me very soon!

You can start your adventure on Page 1.

**211**

A new month has just passed. Add any income from your buildings to your Bank Account in your Ledger. If you have various end-of-month bonuses, don't forget to count them.

**212**

Are you really this kind of man? It's a good thing someone came to distract you, giving the cat time to escape. Regardless, the cat's owner saw you and decided to leave Your Town. Your population drops by 1 and your Approval drops by 5 points. Go back to your office in 88... and don't you dare try anything like this again!

**213**

The Farmer's Market was an incredible success, Mister Mayor! The selection of produce is varied and residents from neighboring towns are now stocking up here. It's revenue has far exceeded our expectations. It now earns us an additional $100 per month.

After noting down all of this, go back to 88. As you know, you won't be able to visit the engineer until another month has passed.

**214**

But don't you worry about it, Mister Mayor. The sheriff and his deputies are taking care of the situation. Everything should be back in order shortly.

And, as promised, a few days later the situation is even better as your Safety rating goes up 5 points. More travelers are coming in and your Train Station now generates an income of $500 per month. In addition, two new esteemed residents have moved in, including a judge. Return to 88 after taking note of these changes.

**215**

I'll tell ya...somefin', gringolito... what a city like ours really... I mean really needs? Ferpectly fimple...safety, son. Tell you somethin' else.... you build a **Large Sheriff's Office**, and I'll...werk for YOU! Yes sir. When it's done, come see me -HIC- in 197.

It is time to leave your slightly drunken host and head back to your office in 88. Up to you to consider whether his offer is serious or not, and whether you'll decide to build a **Large Sheriff's Office**.

**216**

If you have a loaded weapon, hold your pencil 6 inches above the animal and drop it. If you hit it, go to 106. Otherwise, head to 310.

**217**

Over my dead body. I'm happy where I'm at and I got no reason to move to yer hick place. Now get outta mah' store!

You won't get anything from this man. Go out to 202.

**218**

Come on, be reasonable! In this heat, getting inebriated wouldn't be wise. That being said, you can take the full bottle if you want. Go back to 292.

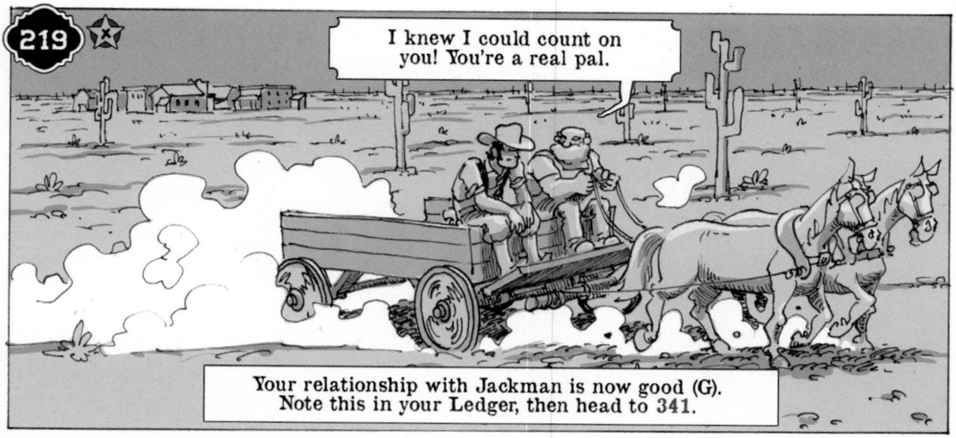
219
I knew I could count on you! You're a real pal.
Your relationship with Jackman is now good (G). Note this in your Ledger, then head to 341.

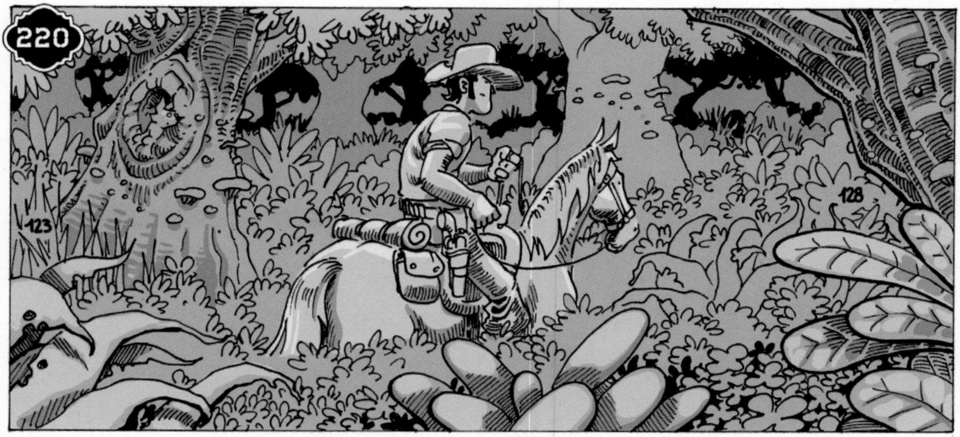
220
123
128

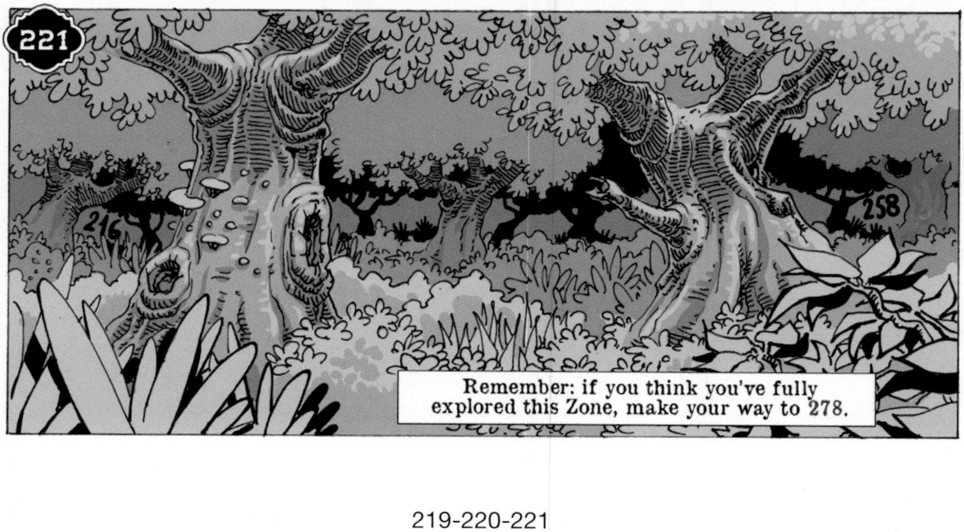
221
216
258
Remember: if you think you've fully explored this Zone, make your way to 278.

You may talk to any person shown in town, but you will only be able to talk to that person once during the game. Once you're done speaking with that person, return to your office. You will have to wait until next month to return to this page, and you can only come here a total of 5 times throughout the game (keep track in your Ledger). When you return to your office, you do not need to note that a month has passed, unless you're told otherwise.

You should count your blessings! While your review was bad, it wasn't bad enough for you them to string you up by the neck. You can start your adventure over with an extra $300, which will help you have a better start.

**THE END**

**225**

No one in sight. Advance to **306**!

**226**

What d'you want, stranger?

If you want to convince this man to come live in Your Town, go to **73**. To ask him if he's got anything to sell, go to **249**. If you suspect a trap and want to draw down on him before he can pull his gun on you, go to **53**. You can also turn back without saying a word in **120**.

**227**

If you want to help this cat *down*, go to 83. If you prefer to *down* the cat (note the subtle difference), head to 212. If you prefer doing nothing, return to 88.

**228**

You can get out of here in 335.

**229**

This is even worse than I thought! Without your help, I will be forced to leave town.

Norman asks you to give him $150 to help him make ends meet. It is up to you whether you will help him or not. In any event, return to 88 after adjusting your Ledger and Bank Account.

**230**

132

**231**

You baffle me, Mister Mayor...

Your decision to ignore this famous doctor has no consequences, at least none that you can see from behind your desk. Return to 88.

**232**

Come on son, keep lookin'! There's gold nuggets over there, I kin tell!

If you can't find any gold, you can head back to the saloon on Page 7 to try your hand at another job.

**233**

You've got yerself a bear skin! Head to 284.

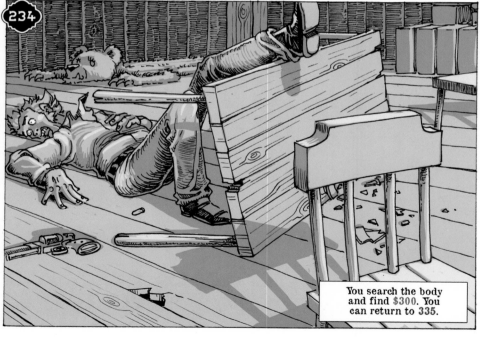

**234**

You search the body and find $300. You can return to 335.

**235**

Your courage causes Your Town to lose 15 points each in both Safety and Approval, in addition to the $1000. You can return to your office in 88.

**236**

The heat makes your head spin, so much so that you no longer know where you're going. Head to 328.

**237**

Not a sec'nd to lose, time to get rich in 232! (heh, I made a rhyme)

If this cave entrance does not inspire confidence, you can turn around and head back to Page 7 to find a new occupation.

**238** ⭐ ❓

A hidden treasure! You find 5 diamonds in this small purse. Note it in your Ledger and then return to where you were.

**239**

You now have the support of everyone in town. You begin your term with an Approval rating of 10. During your adventure, you will meet residents satisfied with how you're managing the town, and others not so much. Each time this happens (satisfaction or disapproval), you must raise or lower your Approval rating.

This rating will have an impact on your adventure. If your citizens approve of your actions, you'll gain advantages. If your Approval rating gets too low, you risk being chased out of town before the end of your term. Now, head to 317.

**240**

You can fire without warning in 151. You can also decide to wait for the man to climb down from his horse and strike up a conversation with him in 318.

**241**

Mister Mayor, have you heard the latest news? One of the most reputable doctors in the state just checked in at our Motel. Rumor has it he's enchanted by the town. What do you think about going to meet him?

If you wish to meet the doctor, go to 198. If this does not interest you, go to 231.

**242**

Well played gringo, well played.

Go to 199 for the last hand.

**243**

Sweet chilli beans 'n dumplin's, how many nuggets d'you bring back?

If you found 67, go to 248.
If you found 68, go to 177.
If you found 69, go to 27.
If none of these match what you have, go to 103.

**244**

WE SHOOT TRESPASSERS ON SIGHT

The sign is not particularly inviting. You can risk it and enter the gate at 117, or turn around and return to your office in 88.

**245**

327

**246**

Mister Mayor, I must say it was very astute of you to extend Sheriff Wallace's office. He personally thanks you, and your relationship with him improves one level. In addition, the population is very happy with this decision and your Approval rating goes up by 10 points. If you've recruited a second qualified sheriff, you receive $500 from a rich and anonymous donor to help you pay his salary.

After writing all of this down, go back to 88. As you know, you won't be able to visit the engineer until another month has passed.

**247**

BLAM!

If you have an Army Fort, the calvary's here to the rescue in 162. Otherwise, go to 66.

**248**

I'm impressed, boy. No junk, only nice, shiny nuggets! You def'nitely deserve this here $700. If ever you need ole' McKenzie's help one 'o these days, just holler!

Your relationship with old McKenzie is now good (G). After noting this in your Ledger as well as the $700 under your Bank Account, head back to the saloon in 282.

**249**

Everything I own fits in this room. In other words, I ain't got much to offer ya.

Truly, nothing interesting. You can go back to 226.

**250**

Evidently, at least three people stopped here. You can continue on your way to 172, or turn back in 49.

**251**

The Casino owner gave you a brief description of our man.
Brown hair, strong build, in his thirties. If you really can't
find him, go back to your office in 88. And sadly, the Casino
and your town will have lost $300.

**253**

Now there's progress for Your Town! You can return to your office in 88.

**254**

The heat makes your head spin, so much so that you don't know where you're going. Go to 328.

236

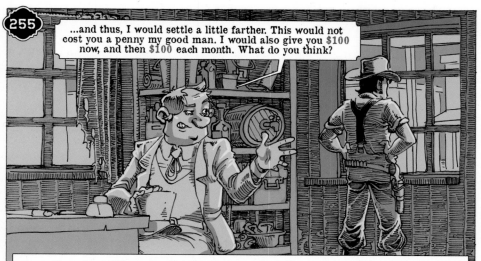

**255**

...and thus, I would settle a little farther. This would not cost you a penny my good man. I would also give you $100 now, and then $100 each month. What do you think?

Roger Kouzak, well-known snake oil salesman, wants to rent space in Your Town for $100 per month. This has the advantage of having no building costs since he'll be using his caravan. On the other hand, due to his reputation, he will most likely attract more than dollars. If you accept his offer, add $100 to your Bank Account, gain 2 Approval points, and lose 3 Safety points. After assigning his Snake Oil Stall a spot (1 x 2 squares), go to 88. If you refuse, ask him to leave your office and make your way to 274.

**256**

LAST WATERHOLE FOR A GOOD WHILE

**257** This Colt and star are yours. You're now my deputy. Your first mission will be to find this dirty bandit. Make your way to 181. I've heard rumor that he might be found there.

Write down that you have a Colt (this can be in addition to your starting revolver) and 5 additional bullets.

**258**

Well done! After searching both thugs, you find $300 and a Henry rifle. This weapon has the following characteristics: long range and rapid reload. You can continue to 168.

**261**

It is extremely difficult to continue under these conditions. The heat is overwhelming, and neither you nor your horse can continue without drinking some water first. If you have a water bottle, drink and continue to 321. Otherwise, turn around to 88. A month will have passed, but you can ensure you're better equipped to return to this zone and explore it.

**262**

Wait up... WAIT!

You can meet her in 14, or ignore her and return to your office in 88. Note that this mission does not count as an exploration. Do not check another month in your Ledger.

It would be foolish to go any further. You can return to 335 if you wish to visit Fontbellon Town, or head to 88 if you've already visited (or if you're just not interested).

So, yer looking for work, are ya? I think I got somethin' for ya. Here's the map to this here region. Show me a place where you think I could find some gold. If you can pull it off, you come with me!

Look closely at the region map found at the end of this book. Are you clever enough to find where to go? Otherwise, go to 331.

**265**

You can pick up their bullets (12 bullets total) as well as the money they had ($200). Pointless to chase the other two as they are already far away. You can continue in 251.

**266**

You lose 100 tokens. Head to 277.

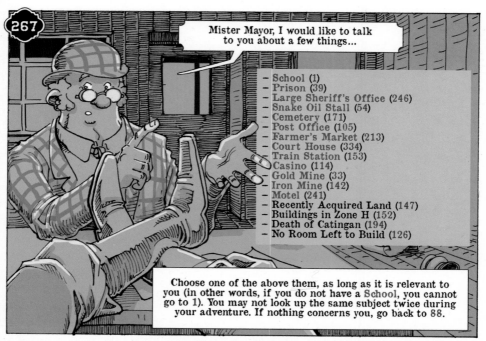

**267**

Mister Mayor, I would like to talk to you about a few things...

- School (1)
- Prison (39)
- Large Sheriff's Office (246)
- Snake Oil Stall (54)
- Cemetery (171)
- Post Office (105)
- Farmer's Market (213)
- Court House (334)
- Train Station (153)
- Casino (114)
- Gold Mine (33)
- Iron Mine (142)
- Motel (241)
- Recently Acquired Land (147)
- Buildings in Zone H (152)
- Death of Catingan (194)
- No Room Left to Build (126)

Choose one of the above them, as long as it is relevant to you (in other words, if you do not have a School, you cannot go to 1). You may not look up the same subject twice during your adventure. If nothing concerns you, go back to 88.

**268**

Alerted by the sound of your gun shot, the owner arrives without warning. Fire the first shot by holding your pencil approximately 6 inches high, then release it on your opponent. If you hit him, go to 121. If you miss or are out of bullets, instead go to 205.

**269**

You can strike up a conversation with the man in 293, or shoot without warning. In this case, you handily kill the man in 234.

**270**

Tips... of course I can give you some. First, don't build too fast. Take the time to think through what adding this or that building means for Your Town. For example, a Bank is great to store your gold, but it also attracts bandits.

You can ask for additional tips in 22 or return to 88 if you do not wish to bother the sheriff anymore.

**271**

Leave my table before I throw you in jail for insultin' the sheriff!

The sheriff no longer wishes to speak to you. Your relationship with him goes from neutral (N) to bad (B). Note of this in your Ledger, then head back to Page 7.

**272**

What do you take us for, worm? Get out of here!

You leave the native camp at triple speed. While fleeing, you drop some of your money and lose $500. Head towards Your Town in 88.

**273**

With a minimum bid of 100 tokens, hands are open. And Mister Frédo wins the game!

You lost. Make your way to 30.

**274**

Bravo, Mister Mayor! Refusing to let that huckster stay in our town is a wise decision. You have my admiration.

Thanks to your decision, your popularity surges and you now have the reputation of being a mayor with an iron fist. You gain 10 Approval points and 5 Safety points. You can return to your office in 88.

**275** We need a Hardware Store, son! This way, I won't need to go all the way to Petoochnook to get my m'terials!

Some interesting information. You can return to 58.

**276** You've been on the road for many days. It's impossible to cross this river. You can choose to enter native territory or go back to your office in 88. In any event, a month passes. Don't forget to note it in your Ledger, and don't forget to take care of your monthly accounting. NOTE: If you decide to return to 88, an additional month will pass.

**277** To tell your real hand and bid 200 tokens more than your starting bid, go to 315. To bluff and bid 200 tokens more than your starting bid, go to 300.

**278** So, what do you think of the land? You can acquire Zone A at no cost if you want to. Regardless, you can return to Your Town in 88.

**279** Hello, Mister Mayor. Pray tell me, would you be so kind as to grant me a private meeting? I have an interesting offer for you.

If you agree to meet with this huckster, make your way to **255**. Otherwise, refuse his request (politely or not, that's up to you), and head to **274**.

**280**

**281**

So, how was yer first day's work?

Stressful!

But I've got a feeling I'm gonna like this town.

As a matter of fact, I'm officially moving here today!

You're obviously very motivated and that's a good thing! Go to 70.

**283** Fortunately, the sheriff intervenes and saves your life. Safety and Approval both go up 1 point. If there is a Doctor's Office or Hospital in your town, you must pay $50 for your treatment. Otherwise, you must get treated in another town, which will cost you $300. You can then return to your office in 88.

**284** I'm afraid you're lost. In any event, your horse is tired and won't be able to go any further. You decide to head back to Your Town in 88.

What a mess... and nothing useful! You can go back out in 146.

**287**

Howdy, stranger! Whadaya buyin'?

If you wish to buy a weapon from him, go to 84. To invite him to come set up shop in Your Town, go to 217. If you prefer to turn back, go to 202.

**288**

Nothing very interesting here, except for this document that will help you identify puma tracks. You decide it is time to return to your office and make your way to 88.

Detail is not your forte, is it?
You still manage to scavenge
16 bullets, $350, and this key.
You can go to 251.

A fine person such as yourself
must deserve a handsome end!

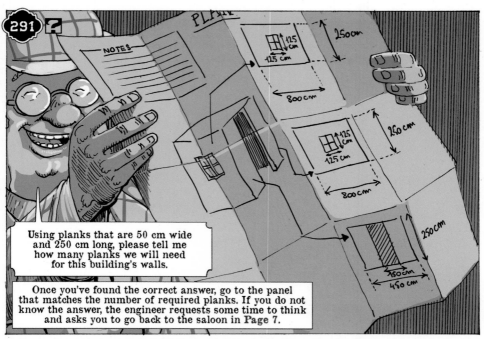

Using planks that are 50 cm wide and 250 cm long, please tell me how many planks we will need for this building's walls.

Once you've found the correct answer, go to the panel that matches the number of required planks. If you do not know the answer, the engineer requests some time to think and asks you to go back to the saloon in Page 7.

291-292

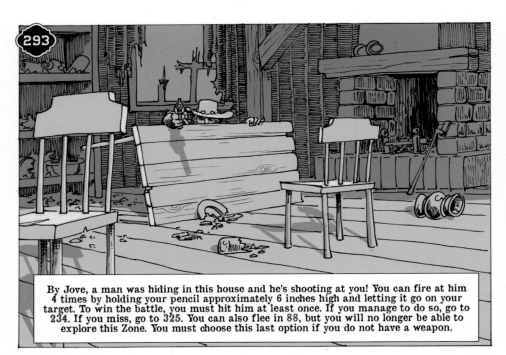

By Jove, a man was hiding in this house and he's shooting at you! You can fire at him 4 times by holding your pencil approximately 6 inches high and letting it go on your target. To win the battle, you must hit him at least once. If you manage to do so, go to 234. If you miss, go to 325. You can also flee in 88, but you will no longer be able to explore this Zone. You must choose this last option if you do not have a weapon.

Here, you see, this is what I'm so proud of, but... I truly need for someone to build a real Cemetery. One day, if you do something about it, I will be truly grateful. In the meantime, come and help me out...

Head to 139.

The tribe chieftain agrees to speak with you in 178, as long as you have not killed any animals during your adventure. Otherwise, he refuses to talk with you and you must return to Your Town in 88.

You lose all of your tokens, except if you had an ace up your sleeve (you must have picked it up previously). In this case, you manage to convince him that it was your card and you win the hand. This leads Fredo to leave town and your Approval goes up 2 points. On the other hand, if you have truly lost, go to 30.

**297**

This magnificent mine is now yours. Sadly, it is exhausted and will earn you only $50 per month instead of the expected $500. Your Approval goes up 4 points and you lose 5 Safety points. You can return to your office in **88** or head back on the road in **333**.

**298**

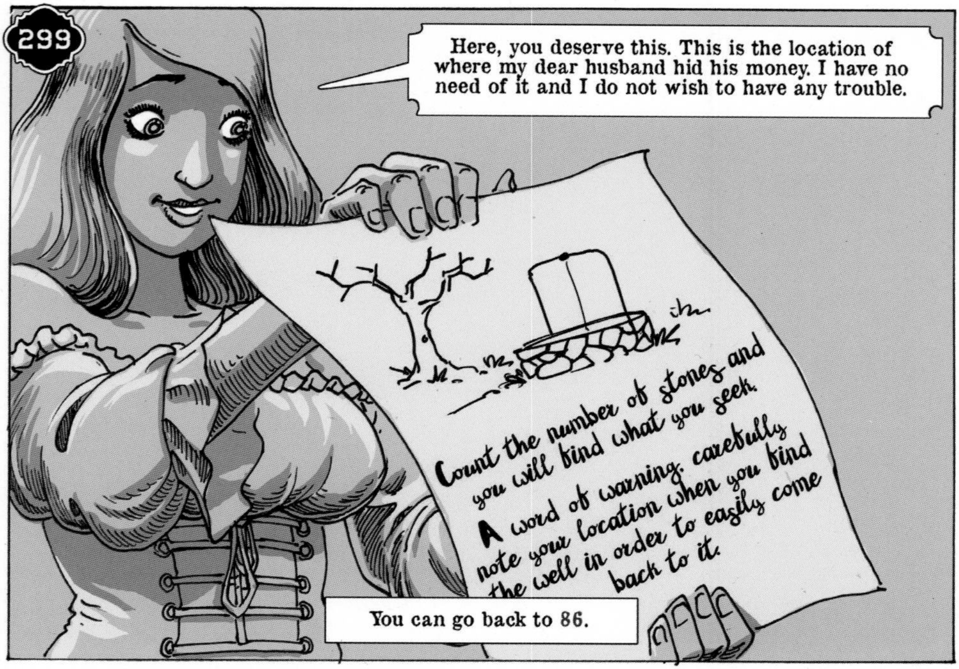
299
Here, you deserve this. This is the location of where my dear husband hid his money. I have no need of it and I do not wish to have any trouble.
Count the number of stones and you will find what you seek.
A word of warning. carefully note your location when you find the well in order to easily come back to it.
You can go back to 86.

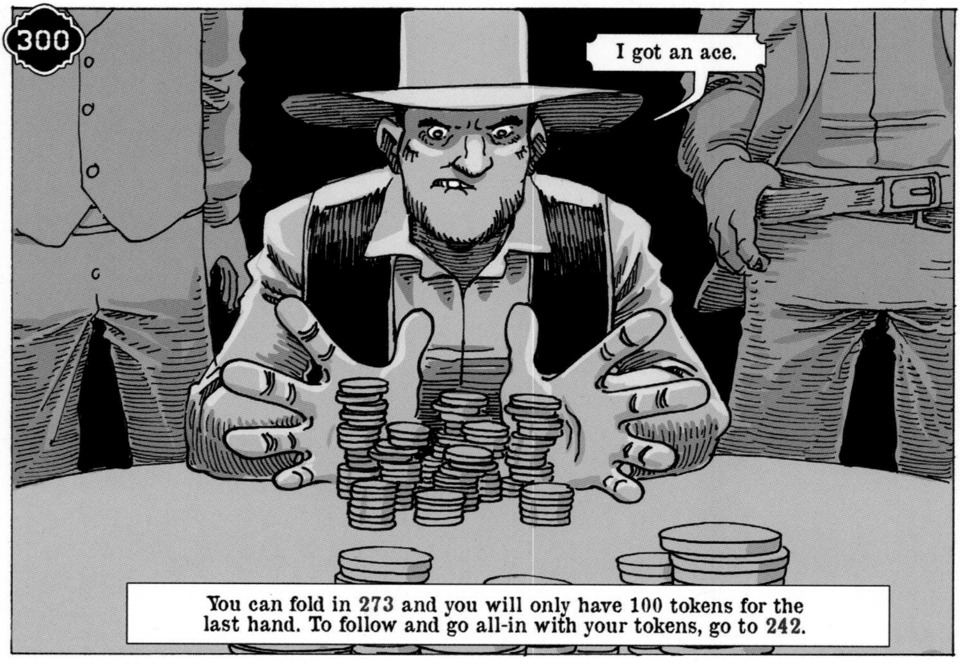
300
I got an ace.
You can fold in 273 and you will only have 100 tokens for the last hand. To follow and go all-in with your tokens, go to 242.

**301** ✦

You can insist and make him an offer in **97**. Otherwise, return to **178**.

**302**

That proposition is... interesting. Okay. I accept. 10 residents of my town will move to Your Town, with the necessary resources to build their homes.

It's your lucky day! You can now add a **Big House** to Your Town without paying a single dollar for it. Even better, among these 10 new residents you find 1 doctor and 1 judge. You can now return to your office in **88**.

**303**

Goodness... I can sell you my land for **$900**.

Non-negotiable!

The decision is yours to make. Regardless, you will then be able to continue to **336** or return to Your Town in **88**.

**304**

Yes, you're right, I do wish to settle here. As a matter of fact, I have a few dollars to my name that might afford me a **House**...

This is rare enough for you to jump on this occasion. This man is offering to pay the building cost of a **Small House**. Thus, you can add one wherever you want. After handling this, head back to **88**.

**305**

You've clearly bothered McKenzie, the prospector, who was focused on counting his gold. Furious with you, he asks nicely that you leave his table. Your relationship with him goes from neutral (N) to bad (B). Note this in your Ledger, then return to Page 7.

**306**

BLAM! BLAM! BLAM! BLAM!

Only one thing left to do: leave this place and return to your office. However, note that a hat as nice as yours costs $50. Deduct this amount from your Bank Account and go to 88.

**307**

After inspecting the makeshift camp and finding three bullets (which will come in handy), you come to the conclusion that one of them must be a prisoner. You stay on your guard. You can continue to 172 or go back to 49.

**308**

Sweet meadow chinchilla, you're the nicest fellow I ever met! Well, you can have this land for $1000. What say ye?

If you accept this offer, Zone F belongs to you. You can build any type of building here. There's a Gold Mine here, but it is dry and won't earn you anything. Your Approval goes up 4 points, but you lose 5 Safety points. Regardless of your decision, you can continue on your way in 333, or return to your office in 88.

I'm afraid your adventure has just ended.

My goodness, you should be ashamed of yourself! Needless to say, people are going to talk about this story. Return to 88, but you lose 5 points each in both Approval and Safety.

312

Natives pendant: $50

Filled water bottle: $50

Rope: $25

Rope: $10

Whiskey bottle: $50

Animal skins: $50

Horseshoe: $50

Horseshoe: $10

Animal bones: $20

Animal claws: $20

Violet flowers: $20

5 bullets: $30

Long-range rifle: $500

Revolver: $200

Diamond: $300

Bundle of 100 wooden logs: $100

Long-range rifle: $200

The blue items can be bought. The green items are those Madam Scott wishes to acquire. If you own some of those items, you can sell them for the price listed in the green box. You may return to 88 at any time.

**313**

As you can see, I received a diploma from the state college and I can teach without any issues. What do you think?

If you have a School, Miss Sarah offers to help as school principal to complete your teaching team and grants you 4 education points. If you have not yet built a school and have the means (and will) to do so, go ahead! You will earn 5 education points and 4 additional points from Miss Sarah. If, however, you consider education to be a sham, or if you do not have the means to start construction, thank Miss Sarah and return to your duties. Regardless, go back to 88.

NOTE: If you decide to hire Miss Sarah, she will settle in your town as an esteemed resident.

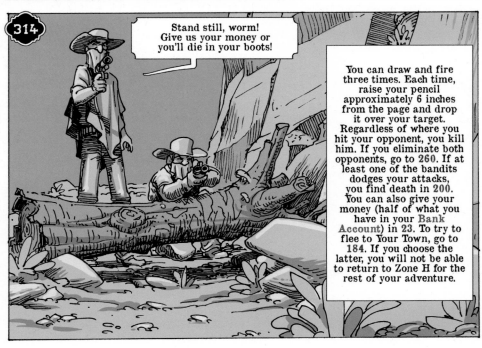

**314**

Stand still, worm! Give us your money or you'll die in your boots!

You can draw and fire three times. Each time, raise your pencil approximately 6 inches from the page and drop it over your target. Regardless of where you hit your opponent, you kill him. If you eliminate both opponents, go to 260. If at least one of the bandits dodges your attacks, you find death in 200. You can also give your money (half of what you have in your Bank Account) in 23. To try to flee to Your Town, go to 184. If you choose the latter, you will not be able to return to Zone H for the rest of your adventure.

313-314

I've got an ace.

You can fold in 273 and you will be down to only 100 tokens for the last hand. To follow and bid all of your tokens, go to 242.

You will need to follow the river in order to find a shallow area and cross it. Go to 170, or turn back and return to your office in 88.

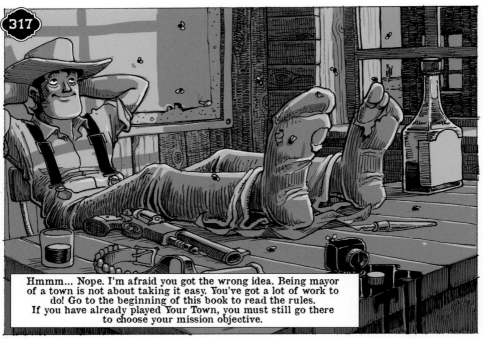

**317**

Hmmm... Nope. I'm afraid you got the wrong idea. Being mayor of a town is not about taking it easy. You've got a lot of work to do! Go to the beginning of this book to read the rules.
If you have already played Your Town, you must still go there to choose your mission objective.

**318**

Give me $1000 and I'll spare you, pup!

To hand him the money, go to 235. You can also choose to shoot, in which case you must hold your pencil approximately 6 inches (above the sheet), aim for the bandit, and let go. If you hit the bandit, you win and go to 151. Otherwise, go to 283.

**319**

If you have a water bottle, take a nice long sip and go to 17. Otherwise, head to 328.

**320**

Hey there friend! What're you doin' on my land?

To let him know that you're interested in purchasing his land, go to 303. To ask him about himself, go to 56. You may also ignore him and continue to 336.

You're saved! You'll be able to quench your thirst and grab a bite. Go to 335.

This puma skin will come in handy later. Note it in your Ledger, under Notes. You can continue on your way in 211, or head back to your office in 88.

What? You really wish to work with me? That's fantastic news! Join me behind the saloon in 294, I've got something to show you.

Herbert did not take kindly to you rejecting his request. He set fire to the buildings found in Zone H. Consequently, you must erase half the buildings, rounded up, found in Zone H (e.g., if you have three buildings, you erase two). You choose which buildings to erase. Then you return to 88.

**325**

I'm afraid this is the end for you! Start your adventure anew.

**326**

So, what brings you here?

To suggest a business proposition, go to 183. To ask him if some of his residents would move to Your Town, go to 42. If you wish to ask him for advice, go to 270. You can also leave the table to return to your office in 88.

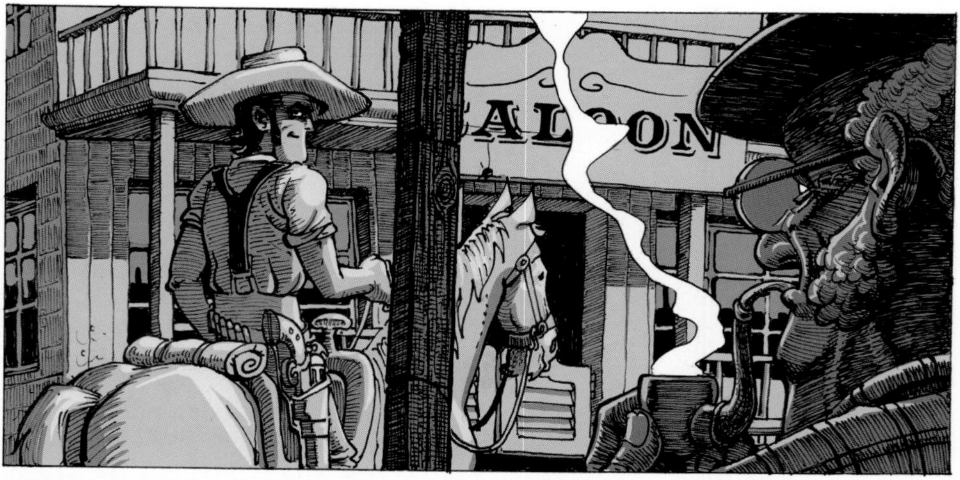
SALOON

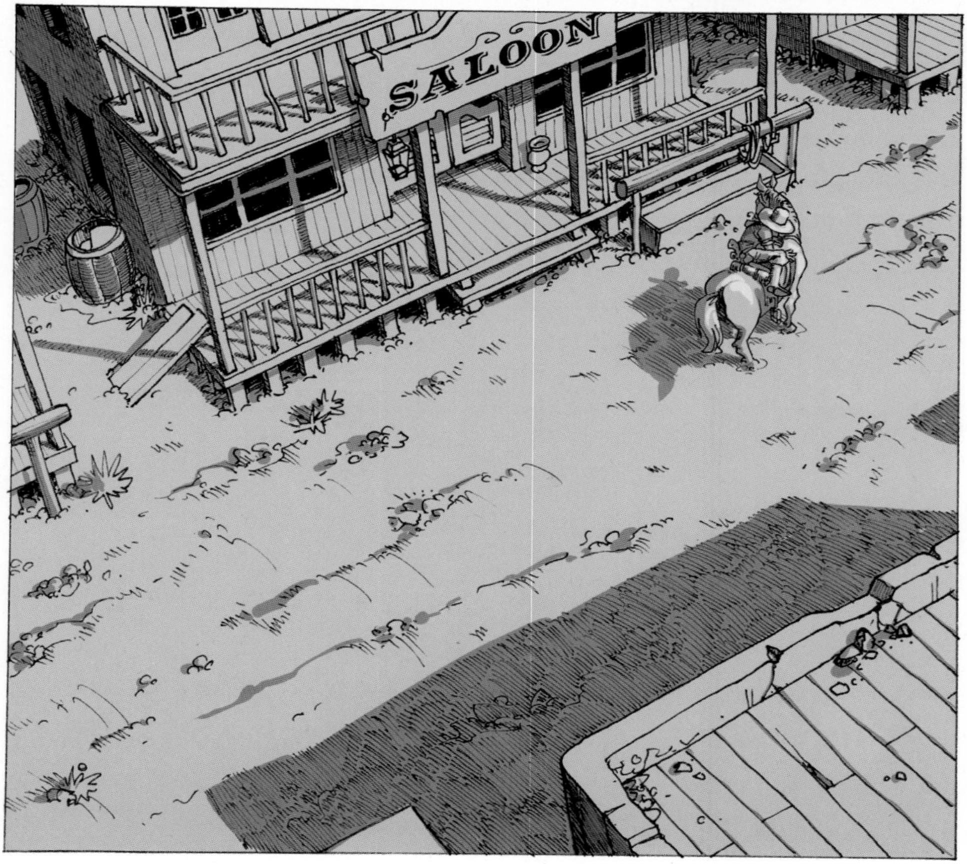
SALOON
SALOON

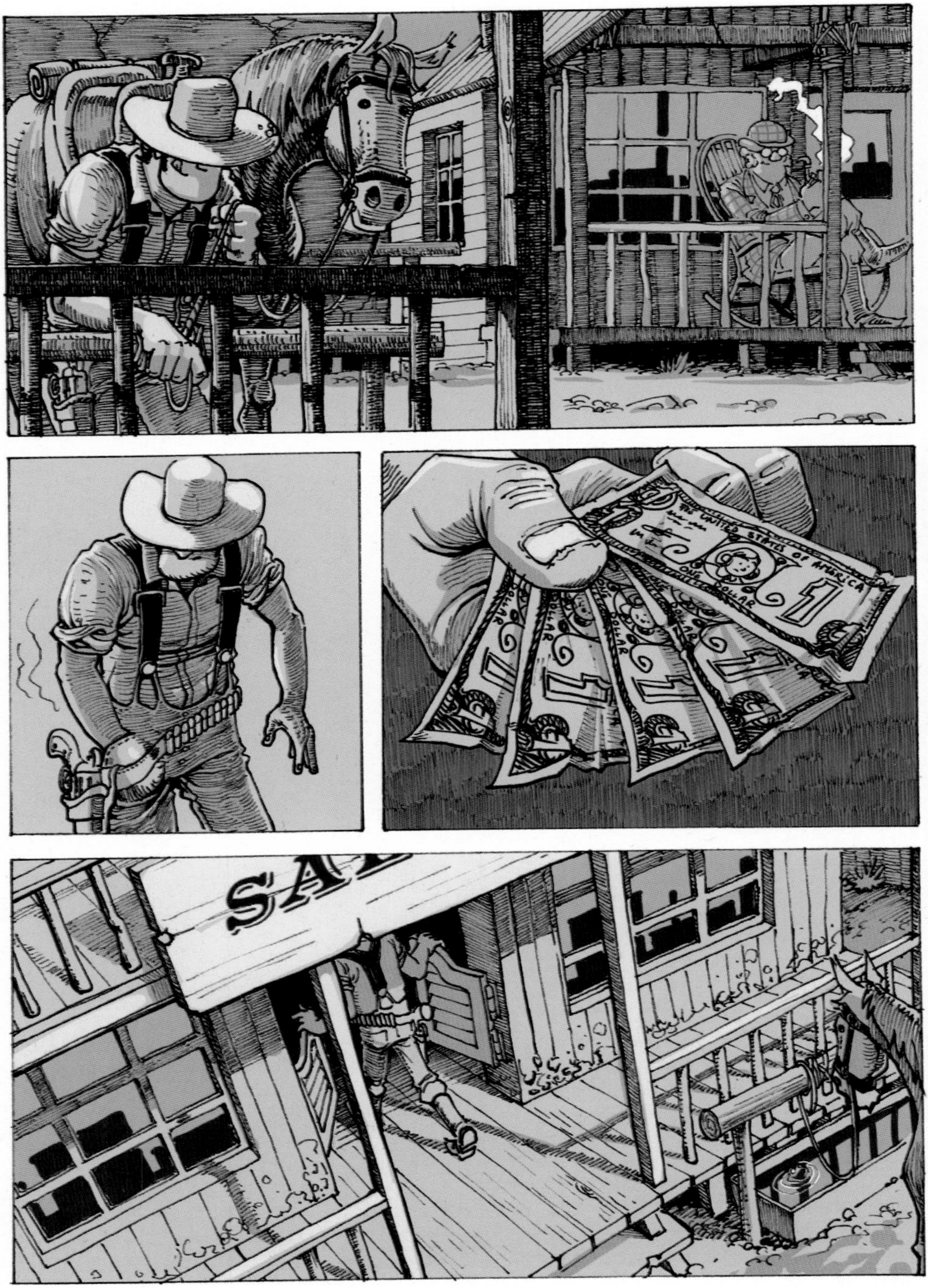
THE UNITED STATES OF AMERICA
ONE DOLLAR

Lucky for you, a man soon crosses your path and brings you safe and sound to 88. However, this experience has traumatized you and you will no longer be able to explore this Zone.

You can get out
of here in 335.

**331**

Not the sharpest tool in the shed, are ya? Then go see the engineer in **47**. Apologies, but I fear you'll slow me down!

**332**

What do you want? Do you seriously think I have time for a pipsqueak of a mayor like you?

If you prefer not to anger the sheriff even further, you can go to your office in **88**. If you wish to make peace with the man, go to **57**. If you wish to enforce your authority, head to **156**.

**333**

**334**

Mister Mayor, the Court House has been full since its construction. So much so that we earn an extra $100, for a total of $400 per month! On the other hand, we must build a Prison immediately, if you have not done so already. If you do not have the financial means to build one, the Court House will close its doors until a Prison is built and you will have to pay $100 to reopen it. Obviously, it will not generate any income while closed.

After noting all of this in your Ledger, go back to **88**. Like each month, you won't be able to visit the engineer until another month has passed.

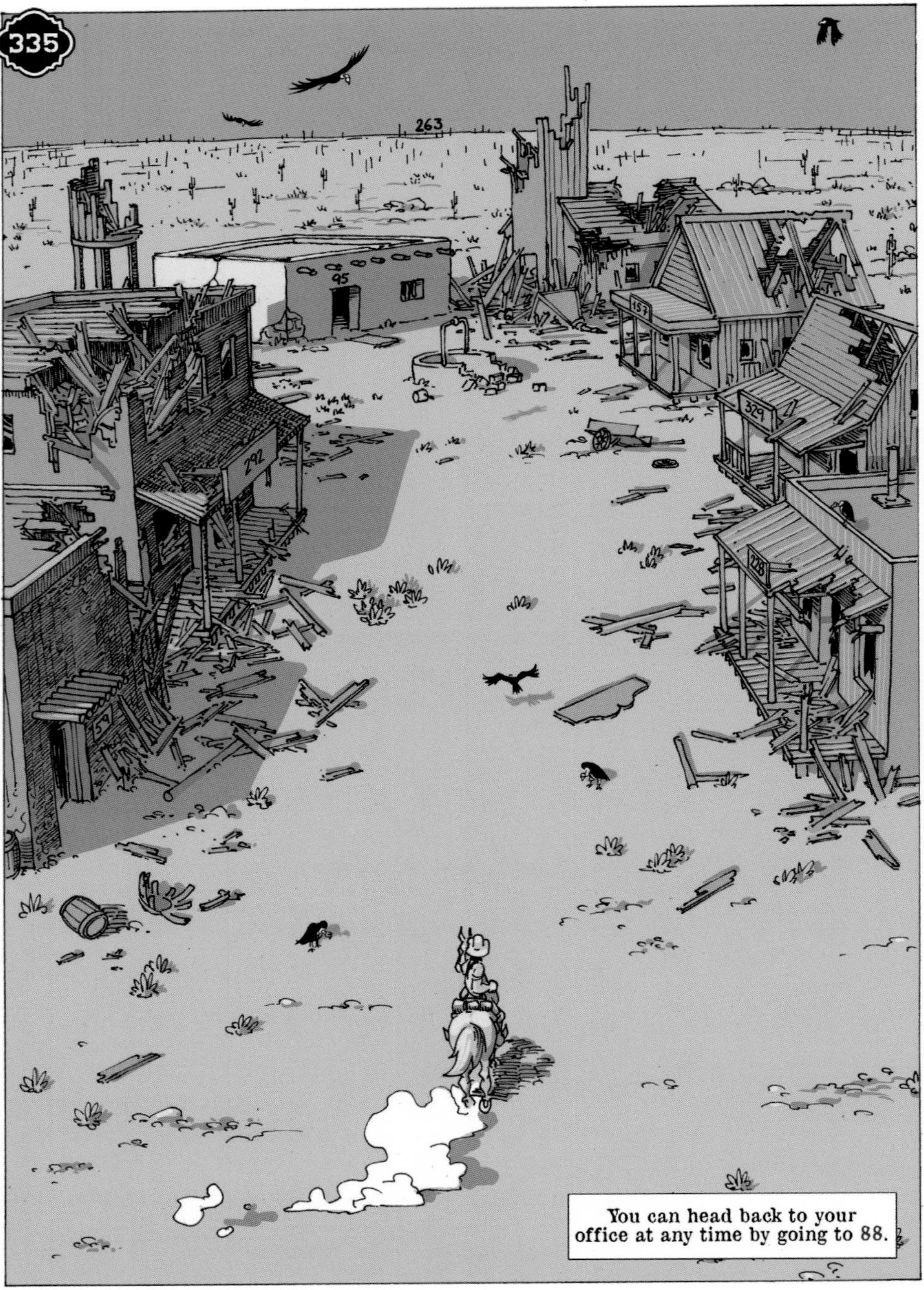
335
263
95
157
329
292
228
59
You can head back to your
office at any time by going to 88.

You can enter this house in 288. Otherwise, turn back and return to Your Town in 88.

**338**

Well, there isn't much to explore around here. You can return to town in 88. You better think long and hard before you buy any land in this area...

**339**

You require assistance? Perfect, that's what I'm here for!

First off, look at the map (I strongly recommend you download it from the **vanrydergames.com** website and print it out).

As you can see, the map is divided into multiple Zones. You are currently in the Zone to the right called "Town Zone." This is where you'll find the saloon, the sheriff's office, and my house. For now, you can build within that perimeter. Don't worry, however, you will have many opportunities to acquire new land as you progress through your adventure.

Other than needing enough money in your Bank Account, the only other requirement for your buildings is that each has at least one side that touches the street, as you can see in the example below.

Did you get all that? Excellent! You can now build your House, which will also serve as your office. Draw it on your map and then return to the saloon in 80.

**340**

You can return to your office in 88.

**341**

The road was long but you are finally back. Before continuing your adventure, don't forget to cash in any money received from bonuses and update your Ledger. Then, head to your office in 2.

# LEDGER

## BANK ACCOUNT

## MONTHLY INCOME

## NOTES

## POPULATION

| | | | | | | | | | |
|---|---|---|---|---|---|---|---|---|---|
| 1 | 2 | 3 | 4 | 5 | 6 | 7 | 8 | 9 | 10 |
| 11 | 12 | 13 | 14 | 15 | 16 | 17 | 18 | 19 | 20 |
| 21 | 22 | 23 | 24 | 25 | 26 | 27 | 28 | 29 | 30 |
| 31 | 32 | 33 | 34 | 35 | 36 | 37 | 38 | 39 | 40 |
| 41 | 42 | 43 | 44 | 45 | 46 | 47 | 48 | 49 | 50 |
| 51 | 52 | 53 | 54 | 55 | 56 | 57 | 58 | 59 | 60 |
| 61 | 62 | 63 | 64 | 65 | 66 | 67 | 68 | 69 | 70 |
| 71 | 72 | 73 | 74 | 75 | 76 | 77 | 78 | 79 | 80 |
| 81 | 82 | 83 | 84 | 85 | 86 | 87 | 88 | 89 | 90 |
| 91 | 92 | 93 | 94 | 95 | 96 | 97 | 98 | 99 | 100 |
| 101 | 102 | 103 | 104 | 105 | 106 | 107 | 108 | 109 | 110 |
| 111 | 112 | 113 | 114 | 115 | 116 | 117 | 118 | 119 | 120 |
| 121 | 122 | 123 | 124 | 125 | 126 | 127 | 128 | 129 | 130 |
| 131 | 132 | 133 | 134 | 135 | 136 | 137 | 138 | 139 | 140 |
| 141 | 142 | 143 | 144 | 145 | 146 | 147 | 148 | 149 | 150 |

## ESTEEMED RESIDENTS

| | | | | | | | | | |
|---|---|---|---|---|---|---|---|---|---|
| 1 | 2 | 3 | 4 | 5 | 6 | 7 | 8 | 9 | 10 |
| 11 | 12 | 13 | 14 | 15 | 16 | 17 | 18 | 19 | 20 |

## APPROVAL

| | | | | | | | | | |
|---|---|---|---|---|---|---|---|---|---|
| 1 | 2 | 3 | 4 | 5 | 6 | 7 | 8 | 9 | 10 |
| 11 | 12 | 13 | 14 | 15 | 16 | 17 | 18 | 19 | 20 |
| 21 | 22 | 23 | 24 | 25 | 26 | 27 | 28 | 29 | 30 |
| 31 | 32 | 33 | 34 | 35 | 36 | 37 | 38 | 39 | 40 |
| 41 | 42 | 43 | 44 | 45 | 46 | 47 | 48 | 49 | 50 |
| 51 | 52 | 53 | 54 | 55 | 56 | 57 | 58 | 59 | 60 |
| 61 | 62 | 63 | 64 | 65 | 66 | 67 | 68 | 69 | 70 |
| 71 | 72 | 73 | 74 | 75 | 76 | 77 | 78 | 79 | 80 |
| 81 | 82 | 83 | 84 | 85 | 86 | 87 | 88 | 89 | 90 |
| 91 | 92 | 93 | 94 | 95 | 96 | 97 | 98 | 99 | 100 |

## GOLD PIECES

| 1 | 2 | 3 | 4 | 5 | 6 | 7 | 8 | 9 | 10 |
|---|---|---|---|---|---|---|---|---|---|

## WANTED OUTLAWS

| 1 | 2 | 3 | 4 | 5 |
|---|---|---|---|---|

## HIDDEN TREASURES

| 1 | 2 | 3 | 4 |
|---|---|---|---|

## VISITS TO TOWN

| 1 | 2 | 3 | 4 | 5 |
|---|---|---|---|---|

## RELATIONSHIPS

| NAME | G | N | B | NAME | G | N | B |
|---|---|---|---|---|---|---|---|
| SHERIFF | | | | | | | |
| NORMAN | | | | | | | |
| McKENZIE | | | | | | | |
| JACKMAN | | | | | | | |
| | | | | | | | |
| | | | | | | | |

## JOBS

| | | | | | | | | | | | | | | | |
|---|---|---|---|---|---|---|---|---|---|---|---|---|---|---|---|
| 1 | 2 | 3 | 4 | 5 | 6 | 7 | 8 | 9 | 10 | 11 | 12 | 13 | 14 | 15 | 16 |
| 17 | 18 | 19 | 20 | 21 | 22 | 23 | 24 | 25 | 26 | 27 | 28 | 29 | 30 | 31 | 32 |
| 33 | 34 | 35 | 36 | 37 | 38 | 39 | 40 | 41 | 42 | 43 | 44 | 45 | 46 | 47 | 48 |
| 49 | 50 | 51 | 52 | 53 | 54 | 55 | 56 | 57 | 58 | 59 | 60 | 61 | 62 | 63 | 64 |
| 65 | 66 | 67 | 68 | 69 | 70 | 71 | 72 | 73 | 74 | 75 | 76 | 77 | 78 | 79 | 80 |

## FOOD

| | | | | | | | | | | | | | | | |
|---|---|---|---|---|---|---|---|---|---|---|---|---|---|---|---|
| 5 | 10 | 15 | 20 | 25 | 30 | 35 | 40 | 45 | 50 | 55 | 60 | 65 | 70 | 75 | 80 |
| 85 | 90 | 95 | 100 | 105 | 110 | 115 | 120 | 125 | 130 | 135 | 140 | 145 | 150 | 155 | 160 |

## SAFETY

| | | | | | | | | | | | | | | | |
|---|---|---|---|---|---|---|---|---|---|---|---|---|---|---|---|
| 1 | 2 | 3 | 4 | 5 | 6 | 7 | 8 | 9 | 10 | 11 | 12 | 13 | 14 | 15 | 16 |
| 17 | 18 | 19 | 20 | 21 | 22 | 23 | 24 | 25 | 26 | 27 | 28 | 29 | 30 | 31 | 32 |

## HEALTH

| | | | | | | | | | | | | | | | |
|---|---|---|---|---|---|---|---|---|---|---|---|---|---|---|---|
| 1 | 2 | 3 | 4 | 5 | 6 | 7 | 8 | 9 | 10 | 11 | 12 | 13 | 14 | 15 | 16 |
| 17 | 18 | 19 | 20 | 21 | 22 | 23 | 24 | 25 | 26 | 27 | 28 | 29 | 30 | 31 | 32 |

## EDUCATION

| | | | | | | | | | | | | | | | |
|---|---|---|---|---|---|---|---|---|---|---|---|---|---|---|---|
| 1 | 2 | 3 | 4 | 5 | 6 | 7 | 8 | 9 | 10 | 11 | 12 | 13 | 14 | 15 | 16 |
| 17 | 18 | 19 | 20 | 21 | 22 | 23 | 24 | 25 | 26 | 27 | 28 | 29 | 30 | 31 | 32 |

## BULLETS

| 1 | 2 | 3 | 4 | 5 | 6 | 7 | 8 | 9 | 10 | 11 | 12 | 13 | 14 | 15 | 16 | 17 | 18 |
|---|---|---|---|---|---|---|---|---|---|---|---|---|---|---|---|---|---|

## HORSESHOES

| 1 | 2 | 3 | 4 | 5 | 6 | 7 | 8 | 9 | 10 | 11 | 12 | 13 | 14 | 15 |
|---|---|---|---|---|---|---|---|---|---|---|---|---|---|---|

## MONTH

| 1 | 2 | 3 | 4 | 5 | 6 | 7 | 8 | 9 | 10 | 11 | 12 |
|---|---|---|---|---|---|---|---|---|---|---|---|

GO TO
PANEL 204

EVENTS
☆ 102

CONSULT
ENGINEER 267

You can download this Ledger from our
website: **www.vanrydergames.com**

# BUILDING REGISTRY

| NAME | RESIDENTS | COST | MONTHLY INCOME | BONUS (UPON BUILDING ONLY) | REQUIREMENTS | APPROVAL |
|---|---|---|---|---|---|---|
| Small House | 1 | $150 | $50 | - | None | 1 |
| Mid-size House | 4 | $300 | $100 | - | None | 1 |
| Big House | 10 | $500 | $200 | - | 5 Small Houses | 2 |

| NAME | JOBS | COST | MONTHLY INCOME | BONUS (UPON BUILDING ONLY) | REQUIREMENTS | APPROVAL |
|---|---|---|---|---|---|---|
| Small Farm | 1 | $150 | $50 | Food +5 | None | 1 |
| Big Farm | 2 | $300 | $100 | Food +20 | 5 Small Farms | 2 |
| Ranch | 5 | $500 | $100 | Food +20 | Big Farm | 3 |
| Stagecoach Station | 1 | $500 | $200 | Esteemed Residents +2 | Ranch | 5 |
| Farmer's Market | 5 | $600 | $50 | Food +50 | 5 Farms (any size) | 3 |
| Grocery Store | 1 | $300 | $50 | Food +20 | 2 Farms (any size) | 1 |
| Hardware Store | 1 | $400 | $100 | Misc. Items | Grocery Store | 2 |
| Doctor's Office | 1 | $200 | $50 | Health +2 | 1 Doctor | 3 |
| Hospital | 5 | $400 | $0 | Health +5 | 1 Doctor | 4 |
| Cemetery | 1 | $500 | $200 | None | None | 1 |
| Blacksmith | 1 | $200 | $50 | Safety +1 | None | 2 |
| Bank | 1 | $300 | $150 | Safety -5 | None | 2 |
| Snake Oil Stall | 1 | $200 | $100 | Safety -1 | None | 2 |

| | NAME | JOBS | COST | MONTHLY INCOME | BONUS (UPON BUILDING ONLY) | REQUIREMENTS | APPROVAL |
|---|---|---|---|---|---|---|---|
| | Post Office | 1 | $100 | $10 | None | None | 2 |
| | Theater | 2 | $400 | $100 | Esteemed Residents +2 | None | 3 |
| | Small Prison | 2 | $200 | -$50 | Safety +3 | Blacksmith | 4 |
| | Large Prison | 5 | $1,000 | -$100 | Safety +10 | Small Prison | 5 |
| | Large Sheriff's Office | 4 | $500 | -$100 | Safety +5 | Blacksmith | 5 |
| | Army Fort | 10 | $800 | -$150 | Safety +20 | Small Prison | 6 |
| | Court House | 3 | $200 | $300 | Safety +1 | 1 Judge | 4 |
| | Town Hall | 2 | $500 | -$200 | Esteemed Residents+1 | Population 30 | 4 |
| | Train Station | 2 | $1,000 | $400 | Esteemed Residents +3 | Carpenter's Shop Iron Mine | 6 |
| | Casino | 5 | $1,000 | $300 | Safety -8 Esteemed Residents +3 | Bank | 4 |
| | School | 2 | $400 | -$100 | Education +5 | 1 Teacher | 4 |
| | Carpenter's Shop | 2 | $200 | $50 100 wood | 100 wood | None | 2 |
| | Motel | 2 | $300 | $150 | Esteemed Residents +1 | None | 2 |
| | Iron Mine | 5 | $50 | $300 | None | Iron Vein | 4 |
| | Gold Mine | 5 | $50 | $500 | Safety -5 | Gold Vein | 4 |
| | Park | 0 | $200 | $0 | None | None | 2 |
| | Skyscraper | 0 | $0 | $0 | None | Special Authorization | 50 |

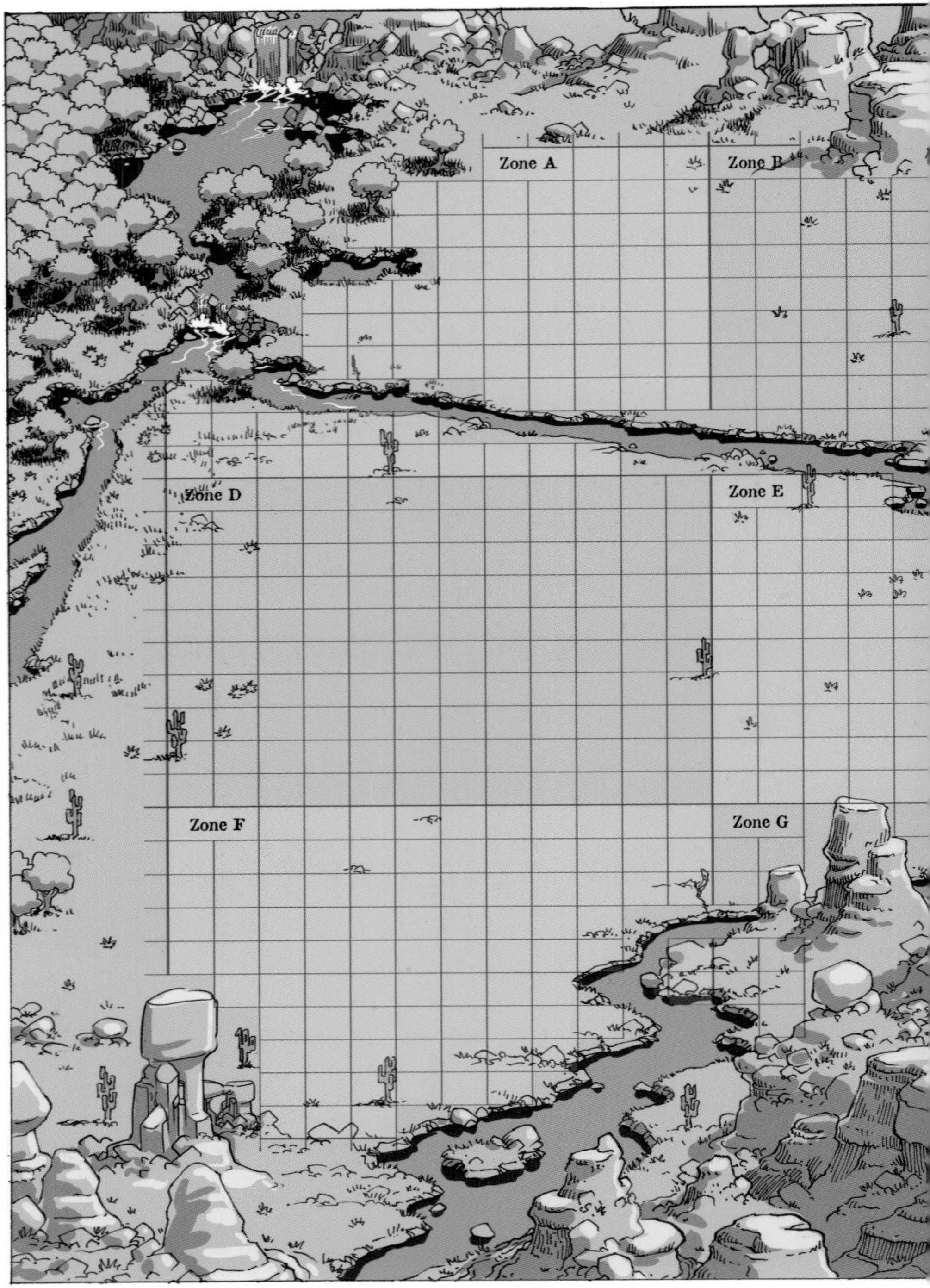
Zone A
Zone B
Zone D
Zone E
Zone F
Zone G